Published by
Franklin-Sarrett Publishers
3761 Vineyard Trace
Marietta, GA 30062-0527
USA
SAN: 297-9918

First Printing 1994
Second Printing 1995
Manufactured in the United States of America

**Library of Congress Cataloging in Publication**
Borden, Kay, 1950-
    Bulletproof news releases : help at last for the publicity
deficient / by Kay Borden.
    p. cm.
    Includes bibliographical references and index.
    Library of Congress 93-72466.
    ISBN 0-9637477-0-3

3 2280 00516 7648

    1. Advertising.  2. Publicity.   I. Title.

HF5804.B67 1993                    659.1

**$18.95 Softcover**

**Cover Design by Sarrett Creative, Atlanta, GA**
**Illustration by Clem Bedwell**

# Contents

# Preface

Among the lately swelling ranks of the small business/entrepreneurial explosion are but two kinds of people: those daring thinkers obsessed with a burning desire down deep in the pit of their bellies to do great things, make a million ASAP, and live and work doing what they want to do at the pace they choose to do it; and the others who joined more reluctantly, forced into membership after the big, hairy corporate monster had an itch and they got scratched. Regardless of which door they came in, the day-to-day job is now pretty much the same -- be the boss, make it work, and find and use every tool available to generate revenue.

When first inspired to write this book, I wanted to produce the best small business guide on news release publicity available anywhere. In the early stages of the project, while working up my marketing plan, I believed I could sell this book as a solution to a problem -- that being the high cost of advertising and the cost of attracting and retaining customers. *If I can get their attention with that, then I can show how promotional news releases stretch ad budgets while capturing a widely circulated, impartial, respected third party's seal-of-approval for their business activities.*

But after talking to a few friends I realized many small business operators have no concept of news release publicity, much less how to use it. Sharp individuals, well-armed for success -- those who know about financing, making a weekly payroll, capital investments, taxes, cash flow, selling, and advertising -- didn't know what I was talking about. Gene, a young chiropractor with two clinics and a full page ad in the Nashville, TN yellow pages, said, '*Oh, you mean contro-versy?*' Sarah, whose husband Rick is a manufacturers' rep, said, '*He already knows everybody he sells to*'. And entrepreneur Jan, with a flavored shaved ice stand, just sort of squinted at me with her mouth hanging half open and said nothing. I had to change my approach.

The intent is not to suggest that news releases alone constitute a complete marketing approach, but rather to explore it comprehensively as one facet of the overall marketing plan (though a fundamental one because of its impact on the success of other promotional activities). So, from presenting a solution to a problem I discovered few knew they had, I moved instead to reintro-ducing an old tool, invaluable for its business benefit, though practiced little and almost never properly undertaken. Just how I would actually accomplish this came to me in one of those forehead slapping moments when one realizes simple brilliance and in the same instant wonders why it hadn't occurred to you sooner.

As a consequence, you are holding the first-ever small business promotional tool compiled with the aid of its victims. Poor journalists have suffered long enough and, when asked, were more than candid about their frustrations and the condition of the publicity game in general. The resulting revelations are so much the better for the many small business owners choked off from opportunity because they "can't see the forest for the trees." I surveyed 135 professional American journalists strictly on the subject of small business news releases, and they responded with heartfelt and sometimes blunt advice.

I intended for the survey to validate the other material in this book, and to that end I hope I have treated the responses fairly and in the proper context. The lessons attempted about news release publicity go way past just saying "do it", past the simple mechanics of formatting, past how to produce meeting and job promotion announcements, past any skimming, broad brush treatment to the "meat and potatoes" *heart* of the issue -- the stuff real editors want from the editors themselves. For the uninformed, I hope the idea behind the survey becomes clear and points the way to a new window of opportunity. For the misinformed, I hope it drives out any previous notions about so-called free advertising and sets a new path. For the journalists, I hope I've done my job and the message gets through. The completed survey from Tina Kunkler, editor of *The LaRue County Herald News* in Hodgenville, KY included a nice letter which began, "I want to thank you first for asking these questions and writing this book. News releases have always been a pet peeve of mine." And before ever seeing the finished product, Mike Stepanovich, business editor of *The Bakersfield Californian*, said, "You're doing a great service for people like me." I know you all agree to the need.

Here's hoping.

Kay Borden
January 1994

# About the author

Kay Sarrett Borden is a senior information services representative with Lockheed Aeronautical Systems Company and head of Franklin-Sarrett Publishers in Marietta, GA. The former journalist, a 1972 graduate of Georgia Southern College, began her newspaper career as a reporter with *The Coffee County Progress* in Douglas, GA, and was promoted to associate editor before moving to *The Blackshear Times* in Blackshear, GA as news editor. She also served as news editor for *The Cherokee Tribune* in Canton, GA before joining Lockheed's Service Manuals Publication Division as an editor. She and husband Tom, a senior quality systems auditor with Lockheed, make their home in Marietta.

# Acknowledgments

I am sincerely grateful for the contributions of the 135 newspaper professionals from around the country who played such a huge part in making this book possible. Their input proved an invaluable window into newspapers of the nineties and, if I've done my job, the advice and opinions of these journalists will perhaps help to open up the media to small business people so obviously bewildered by it. Personally, I couldn't wait to get to the mail box each day, and delighted in opening and reading each response, and, in many cases, the accompanying notes and letters. Thanks for generously giving of your time, thanks for your thoughtful and sometimes lively comments, and most of all, thanks for caring. I tried to do your material justice. I hope you find the ultimate treatment, if not entirely pleasing, at least accurate and fair.

To book author and magazine editor Jimmy Jacobs, I am forever indebted for his thoughtful critique of the manuscript. Life is funny. Years ago I met Jimmy and his brother R.L. while playing volleyball at the church gymnasium as teenagers. And though we went our separate ways (ironically, all to study journalism), I later "caught up" with Jimmy when on my very first day as a Lockheed "new hire," R.L. was reintroduced as a coworker.

Last spring, while heavy into this project, I found Jimmy again after he appeared on local television promoting his first book, *Trout Fishing in North Georgia*. Jimmy is editor of *Georgia Sportsman*, *Florida Game & Fish,* and *Alabama Game & Fish* all headquartered in Marietta, GA. (Jimmy has the Perfect Job: He likes to write and he likes to fish so he writes about fishing.) I also must give Jimmy credit for the "bulletproof" title.

I was led to John F. Budd, Jr., by contributing editor Robert A. Hatch. Mr. Budd, chairman and CEO of Omega Group, New York and author of *Street Smart Public Relations*, generously shared his thoughts about business news release publicity formulated over years in the public relations business.

Coworker Doug Oliver handles all media relations for maritime patrol aircraft programs for Lockheed Aeronautical Systems Company, and he graciously agreed to read the manuscript from a "big business" view. Doug enduring a stint as a newspaper business and political writer of which he laments, "I hated it. I got all these press releases from all these businesses that said 'how great my business is.' *Bulletproof News Releases* contains useful advice for any business person." Thanks, Doug.

I wish I had found author and business consultant Robert Hays earlier in the project. By the time I asked him to look over the manuscript, the book was too far along to incorporate most of his valuable suggestions, though rest assured future revisions will certainly benefit from them. However, his meticulous reading turned up a number of technical errors I *was* able to correct for this printing. In addition to serving as a consultant to more than a hundred companies and agencies, Hays has written four books and more than 150 published articles.

Former publisher of *Georgia Trends* Magazine and small businessman Clint Smith is responsible for **Chapter Key Points** at the end of each section. As he so aptly pointed out, some sort of summarization was needed, especially for the busy marketing manager who may only scan the material to determine its merit before passing it on to a staff person. Thanks also goes to Clint for suggesting I talk to Otis White and then arranged the meeting. Otis' expert overview gave me yet another reader's perspective from which to judge the material.

My first cousin Joel Sarrett, whose company Sarrett Creative in Atlanta, GA designed the cover, obliged me with a "family reading" of the manuscript, and made some valuable suggestions including also pointing out the need to summarize. I'm grateful for all the excellent help with the cover, and especially want to thank Designer Christopher Rossi for his unflappable toleration of me. Nice job, guys.

To all of these very busy individuals who so generously made time for me, I am forever in your debt.

And last, because I owe him the most, my husband Tom who endured, as he puts it, as a 'computer widower' without much complaint. Thanks. I love you.

*Dedicated to my parents, George and Caryl.*

# 1

# Myths & Misconceptions

- **Publicity for the '90's**
- **Hiring PR help**
- **Why just newspapers**

News release publicity is dead. Though many promotion-minded business owners and hired public relations help still waste time and money mailing out poor imitations, what is more telling and to a surprising degree, huge numbers of entrepreneurs and small business people *don't know* to use news releases. Newspaper editors, resigned to the loss some years back, find no use for the former and have neither the time nor a spirited commitment to try and educate the latter. Pity. It could have been a beneficial arrangement for them both.

According to those ultimately charged with evaluating and selecting news releases for publication, today's

*"The days of reprinting press releases are long since gone or should be. We use them as tips or story ideas."*

Don Nicoson, Business Editor
**The Arizona Republic**
Phoenix, Arizona

business environment suffers from an abundance of publicity seekers attempting a job for which they demonstrate a woeful lack of training. Incredibly, it's not only the do-it-yourselfers who fall short, but many of those hired to publicize fail miserably.

Robert A. Hatch, formerly with the public relations agency Carl Byoir & Associates, says Byoir client material reached its intended audience because newspaper trained professionals had the final ok; a simple and successful system, albeit as he puts it, a "somewhat tyrannical" one.

Says Hatch "We prided ourselves in putting out publicity materials to the media that the media could use. Everyone at Byoir had been a newspaper reporter or editor or wire service or magazine professional for five or more years before we jumped the traces. The agency even had a copy editor (a former [Associated Press] editor) who had the right to reject releases, no matter how badly the client wanted them put out in a specific form."

Hatch goes on: "I mention all this because the quality of news release writing, indeed the quality of the ideas and quotes that go into [news releases], has fallen way off in the past 10 years. I hardly ever get a release, even from a major agency, that contains a lead that could be used as written. Often they look as if they were produced by a junior sales promotion writer or, worse still, the ad manager of the client firm. Each of these disciplines has a legitimate approach to conveying a commercial message, but neither of them speaks in the language of the news writer."

Hatch's comments are particularly revealing since, as editor and publisher of *The Lakeville Journal*, Lakeville, CT, he's now the object of many contemporary PR writers' appeals.

We might speculate that news release writers believe the media are becoming more stupid with each passing year, and thus unable to spot advertising when they see it (though by what we see broadcast on television and reported in some printed rags, it suggests the loss of brain cells is presumed confined to the public). On the other hand, we could theorize the drop off in quality news releases over the last decade can be linked to the small business explosion and, if we can take a cue from the recent past and forecasts for the future, we must further assume the condition will only worsen as downsizing in the nineties continues.

## Publicity for the '90's

While some media seem hell-bent on dragging out every shock-producing tactic ever invented to get our attention, it's no wonder operators of ordinary small businesses never consider news media coverage as a palatable item to include on their promotional plate. Those who do entertain the idea can become quickly discouraged at the thought of competing with today's headlines. It becomes perfectly understandable, then, why a clothing store owner, eager to jump into the promotional arena and come up with an angle suited to the nineties, may twist things just a bit. In his misguided mind, a new line of street-length dresses might become "dresses for street walking."

*"I wish I had a fraction of the money that's been wasted on mass-mailings of totally irrelevant news releases, or pure advertising. Big agencies are the worst. They must think small town papers are all run by bumpkins."*

Robert M. Williams, Jr.,
Editor & Publisher
*The Blackshear Times*
Blackshear, Georgia

Who could blame the dry cleaner for mentally musing over his fantasy news release entitled "Man Drops Pants?" And a publicity-minded hot dog vendor might imagine a story proclaiming "we relish your buns."

You're probably wondering where you fit in all of this. You're just one person working 16 hours a day trying to make a living; how can you garner news space when you can't possibly compete with the headlines? What's more, you don't want any part of it if getting coverage means manufacturing racy material.

While it's true that shock media -- if it bleeds, it leads -- disturbs even seasoned journalists, less sensational matters occupy a sizeable portion of available news space each day. These refreshing stories sprinkled throughout every edition of every newspaper in the country keep us sane, and many of them tell of ordinary business people just like you. The result is extraordinary publicity. It takes a thoughtful approach, but not only is it possible for entrepreneurs and small businesses to get their share of the headlines, it's very probable and profitable.

Fact is, most small businesses limp around -- promotionally deficient and advertising poor. Though the material in this book cannot identify how you are unique, it can help you spot uniqueness in yourself. It doesn't take much effort to get the public's attention if you can support claims of startling technological advances, phenomenal growth, or an altogether unusual approach to some aspect of business. Since these kinds of headline-making accomplishments

*"PR professionals should spend time learning more about newspapers - they get paid to be effective but often don't get the training."*

Julie M. Vosberg,
Managing Editor
**The Newton Kansan**
Newton, Kansas

aren't likely for Pigpen's Laundry & Dry Cleaning or Adam and Eve's Rib Shack, the material in this book is specifically designed to show you how to use the more mundane aspects about your business to gain no-cost/low-cost media exposure, and either reduce your advertising budget or make it go farther.

With the help of 135 professional American journalists, you will be introduced to a whole new way of thinking about your business activities and how you can take advantage of them to build a reputation, increase customer traffic, and ultimately affect the bottom line in a positive way.

Perhaps you've done some reading about business promotion that included a couple of paragraphs or even a page or two about promoting with news releases. During my search of currently available material on the subject, I was struck by the vagueness of such well-meaning recommendations as "try to get your local newspaper to run a news release about your business." This so-called advice conjures up all sorts of images, from trickery to attempted bribery to a pitiful display of unabashed begging. Equally appalling are such declarations as "newspapers are eager to give their readers news about your products and services" -- another empty statement producing more questions than answers. While both are essentially valid suggestions, they're also meaningless since neither tells even a fraction of the full story.

Since there really is no free lunch, you can't think of news release publicity as free advertising. This implies getting something for nothing. Think of it instead as a fair trade -- exchanging useful

*"Releases are just the beginning. We usually rewrite from there and the writers should not be surprised if we do."*

John Sullivan,
Editor & Publisher
*The Livingston Enterprise*
Livingston, Montana

information for valuable exposure. And since news releases cost you *practically* nothing -- a little time, stationery, and postage -- including them in your marketing plans is fiscally a very sound move when compared with relying on paid advertising alone.

## Hiring PR help

Even if you prefer not to actually do the news release writing yourself, this book will help you to evaluate the performance of a hired professional. By knowing what's expected, you'll be better prepared to judge a candidate's merit before you commit. Whether you contract with a free-lance writer or hire a public relations firm, being familiar with these guidelines ensures you'll get your money's worth. When interviewing a prospective free-lancer or PR firm, weed out the wannabees by asking to see recently *published* samples of news releases composed for other clients. It may seem odd to ask that of so-called professionals in the public relations field, but a number of surveyed editors ranked material from PR firms as low as any received for usefulness and overall writing quality.

Several surveyed editors lived past lives doing PR work, and more than one expressed disbelief at what arrives as agency-produced material. Be sure to ask to see tear sheets or copies of published releases. Don't be persuaded by a pile of neatly typewritten releases ready to be mailed as proof a PR writer can produce. If it hasn't been published, it doesn't count. Be especially leery of a promised 100-publication mailing (or 1,000 or 10,000). Don't be swayed by

*"Press releases seldom run as written. They usually serve to alert staffers to a news story or community issue."*

Michael R. Montgomery, Editor
**The Alton Telegraph**
Alton, Illinois

grand numbers and the 'shotgun effect' theory behind mass-mailings. On the contrary, someone with published samples and an offer to get your message in one or two area newspapers or a dozen pertinent, highly targeted publications actually paints a much more reasonable expectation and becomes the wiser choice. By the time you have finished reading this book, you'll know why.

Not to cast an unflattering light over the entire public relations profession, but the opinions of journalists certainly cannot be discounted (after all, they decide who receives coverage), and it's to your advantage to know enough to protect your own interests.

Highly respected public relations professional John F. Budd, Jr. calls news releases ". . . the oxymoron of our times! They are neither news nor do they release (say) anything -- mostly." Budd, chairman and CEO of Omega Group in New York City and author of *Street Smart Public Relations*, shared a letter with me he sent to the editor of the *Journal of Corporate Communications*, The Medill School of Journalism, Northwestern University, regarding a recent article in the journal about quality in corporate news releases.

"The author completely misses a priceless opportunity to address one of the most troubling issues in communications. He suggests quality is important but perhaps not now. Wrong, wrong, wrong! I can think of ten specific criteria, each of which -- and all of which -- are a quality factor.
1. Writing -- is it pedestrian or professional? This is not a niggling point. The abysmal state of copy is a constant source of irritation to editors. Ask one.

2. Grammatical accuracy -- self-explanatory.

3. Relevance -- is it of legitimate interest to whomever it is being directed? Too many releases are written for the boss, not the ultimate audience.

4. Does it have substance? Are you saying anything? You'd be surprised at the meandering, pointless copy produced in the name of a news release.

5. Level of creativity -- run of the mill or interesting?

6. Proactive or reactive? Not a small point, effectiveness in communication is enhanced by taking the initiative; reactive writing is almost always seen as defensive.

7. Presentation -- is it clean, crisp copy on paper, centered with good margins, no strikeovers or white-outs. Is the release paper unadorned with logos and claims of NEWS dominating?

8. Credibility -- are statements supported by facts? Are sources of attribution credible?

9. Timeliness -- is it hard news or soft? Does the writer know the difference -- and what it means in the writing.

10. Factual accuracy -- self explanatory but a maxim violated often."

An eight-time recipient of the public relations profession's equivalent to the 'Oscar,' Budd learned early in his career that speaking the "language of the news writer" ensured success -- so much so, his then employer's copy was accepted by the media carte blanche, a credential worth looking for during your search for public relations help.

When considering PR candidates, a local media reporter can sometimes be persuaded to do a little free-lance work which should guarantee your

*"Almost all 'news releases' . . . are actually attempts to get advertising without paying for it. We frequently run news stories from our advertisers but never from those who are not, particularly from those who do their advertising in other places or media."*

Norman Grissom, Publisher
***The Mitchell Tribune***
Mitchell, Indiana

material gets used by at least his or her employer. Whomever you choose, consider one of two arrangements. You can agree for that person to act as your representative; he or she becomes the contact should the media call for more information. Or you can hire a ghostwriter so that all material arrives at its destination with every indication you composed it yourself. If the writer is more accessible than you, and you feel comfortable with the individual as your spokesperson, you may benefit by allowing them to act as your agent. It's strictly a matter of personal preference and will make no difference whatsoever to the receiving publication.

Choosing to go with a PR firm or free-lancer runs another risk -- you miss the benefits of doing the releases yourself. You miss the process that stimulates your mind and makes you think about your business, and all the new things you'll learn about yourself and it. You miss the added dimension that brings about new discoveries, ideas for solving problems, and better ways to market, grow, and prosper. These things can only happen when *you* sit down to write.

## Why just newspapers

Concentrating your promotional effort on newspapers, at least initially, does several things. First, it forces you to focus on the one medium where you're likely to reap the greatest benefits. Second, TV and radio news gatherers read newspapers for leads, so it's possible to also hear your item on radio the day it comes out in the paper. And third, newspaper items go into more detail, can be reviewed, passed around, placed in a reference file, or prominently displayed as a reminder with a refrigerator magnet. You can't do that with anything on the airwaves.

## Chapter Key Points

• The best news releases use the "language of the news writer."
• Refer to Budd's 10-Point Quality Checklist on pages 1-7 and 1-8.
• Read this book before hiring professional PR help.
• Stick to newspaper publicity in the beginning.

# 2

# To Market, To Market

- **Advertising that's virtually free**
- **Making sure customers think of you**
- **The right image**
- **Watch for trends**

Running a small business is every bit as multifaceted as running a large corporation, although the limits on time and the resources of one person or a small staff means choosing more carefully how those resources are best spent. Take marketing, for instance. More than just selling, it's systematically ferreting though the entire human race to find the exact group of people most likely to buy your product or service, then making sure they know about you, what you sell, and how you and your products differ from the competition. When it's time to buy, the magic element that actually secures the sale may be what you stand

*"I realize the release is trying to 'sell' something, but the writer should refrain from going overboard on extolling the virtues . . ."*

Dan Bender, Editor
***Greenfield Daily Times***
Greenfield, Ohio

for rather than where buyers have to go to get it or what it costs.

Marketing, now an umbrella term for any activity that makes the cash register ring, no longer just goes along for the ride in today's American business; it's firmly in the driver's seat. And while no single marketing activity will do a complete job, combining several activities at the same time, over time, produces the best results.

A good marketing plan outlines a carefully selected target market, identifies its needs, and lists products

### what business are you really in?

and services to meet those needs. It describes ways to make it easy for potential customers to buy what you sell at affordable prices, establishes your company image, and describes how you intend to let potential customers know you exist. Your marketing plan should reflect sales goals and an outline of the steps necessary to achieve them.

Just as driving from Sarasota to Spokane without a road map would be a frustrating, time-wasted journey of wrong turns and backtracking, so too would any attempt at running a business without a guide. Don't make the mistake of thinking that an organized marketing plan is only for those with the time and resources for that sort of thing. If you are already in business and don't have a marketing plan, stop right now and prepare one. A multitude of excellent material can be found in bookstores and at the local library to guide you.

Perhaps you're just beginning to plot a business strategy. Either way, don't fall into the I-don't-need-to-write-it-down-it's-all-in-my-head trap. No matter how good your head is, you'll lose focus without a written plan. Without putting enough time and thought into what you're doing to write it down, you could find yourself not fully knowing what business you're really in. Sounds utterly preposterous, doesn't it?

Tom, a friend, wanted to produce and distribute a monthly publication designed to supplement high school foreign language classes. He developed a newsletter format and filled it with text and illustrations on contemporary topics of interest to American teens.  Fluent in several languages and knowledgeable enough of desktop publishing methods, he produced the camera-ready pages himself. To solicit subscriptions, Tom developed a direct mail piece that included a sample of the French version newsletter, sales literature and order form, and sent the package to high school foreign language teachers. He also bought small ads in a few specialty magazines read by high school foreign language instructors.

Aware of his activity from the beginning and always interested in progress reports, I frequently found the opportunity to ask how things were going. It was during one of these conversations that I rather offhandedly mentioned the boom in "the mail order business," and how he might be interested in taking a look at a couple of books available at the library on the subject. He looked blank. Tom thought he was publishing educational material, and he was, but he

*"I want to do everything possible to help local businesses, particularly small ones. However, I resent those business owners who expect something for nothing . . ."*

Rhonda Vines, News Editor
***Haralson Gateway-Beacon***
Bremen, Georgia

was trying to sell subscriptions through the mail, and that's mail order. Because Tom was the first to offer such a product, a well-planned news release campaign would have drawn a huge amount of attention and subscriptions before he invested the first dime in direct mail or advertising.

Think through your ideas well enough to understand what business or businesses you're really in, and then write it down. Refer to your plan constantly, change it as often as necessary to match where you are and where you are going -- just don't try to do business without one. In every aspect of business, including promotion and publicity, you must know who you are, what you are doing, and where you are going. With focus and direction, you're best prepared to anticipate potential problems and develop ways to reduce negative impact, to recognize opportunities and methods to take advantage of them, and to mentally compile all the information into a logical, workable plan.

Experts agree lack of focus causes many difficulties in business. The person in charge forgets or never fully knew what the business was all about. It can creep in like extra pounds during the holidays. Left unchecked, you wake up fat one morning and wonder how you got that way. Blurry business owners may notice a problem, but, rather than look for the underlying cause, brush it off as a blip that will correct itself. By the time the significance of the problem hits them, they're in real trouble.

As children we rarely learn either *patience* or *focus*. Many of us manage to enter adulthood without so much as an introduction to these two basic ingredients for successful living. As a result, we flit from one shiny ball to the next in search of enjoyment, work at jobs we don't like, suffer punishing relationships, and become generally unhappy without really knowing why.

I keep myself from drifting with a simple sign. The word "FOCUS" in seven-inch letters is thumb-tacked to the wall just behind my computer. When I glance up from my work, it's what I see. I know this probably sounds a little strange, but I've looked at it so much it now triggers a quick mental check. It reminds me to ask myself *"Am I paying attention."* This helpful synapse has snatched me back from a number of distractions that would keep me from the business at hand. Perhaps it will work for you.

## Advertising that's virtually free

Within every good marketing plan is a section on promotion and publicity outlining indirect and very often inexpensive methods of reaching your target market. Better known as public relations, promotion and publicity do all the good things paid advertising is suppose to do and can be, and many times is, more effective. It's much more subtle than paid advertising yet every bit as necessary. Good public relations simply means communicating openly and honestly and continually with customers and potential customers.

Publicity and promotion is a form or advertising but doesn't announce sales or weekly specials or ask customers to buy. It's much more artful than that. Promotional, nonpaid advertising -- which includes personal sales, displays, trade shows, event sponsorships, brochures, radio and television interviews, newsletters, and news releases -- personalizes your business, creates a public image of the people behind your business name, and gives the buying public a better feeling about doing business with you.

Promotional news releases offer the perfect low-cost avenue of implied endorsement through subtle suggestion. News releases can feature the company's people, how they feel about things, and what they think is important. News releases can be about products or services, but only as they relate to the benefits specific customers receive by using them. If conceived for the right reasons and carried out properly, promotional activities can help establish an allegiance from the buying public approaching that otherwise reserved for God and country.

Practically every publication distributed in the U.S. relies on unsolicited material about people, events, and trends to help fill its pages, and you might as well take advantage of it. The media serving your target market can help potential customers learn about you, and establish your credibility as an expert at what you do. Promoting your business takes a marginal amount of imagination and initiative, but the pay back is more than worth it.

Today every market has a special interest publication or trade association journal. You're no doubt familiar with the ones unique to your own industry. If not,

*"New release preparers need to understand the meaning of the word 'news' and not confuse it with free advertising."*

Mary Valliant, Managing Editor
**Star Democrat & Sunday Star**
Easton, Maryland

you can look them up in the *Encyclopedia of Associations* at the library reference desk.

These business support groups all produce a publication of some kind showcasing member accomplishments and industry news. Participation opens up valuable networking avenues, and information about others within your industry can reveal some noteworthy comparisons. Besides the industry-related benefits, study the publications for format, style, and the type of material they use.

The editors of hundreds of special interest publications search nonstop for information about new techniques, technologies, and trends to satisfy reader appetites, all designed to make their vocation more interesting, more enjoyable, or more profitable. From garbage pickup to gourmet restaurants, a trade magazine exists. Each issue of every publication is devoted to profiles of people just like you pursuing their part of the entrepreneur's American dream. Read these stories of victory over adversity closely and apply "lessons learned" to your own enterprise. Modeling the successes of others in business, known by the fancy term 'benchmarking', is not only legal and ethical but a very smart move. Look for success stories among your competitors. If one or two rivals are eating you alive, why? What are they doing that you're not? When ready to write your own success story, industry publications will want to hear about it.

Positive publicity attracts new customers and cements relations with existing ones. Promotion and publicity first appeared when professional services needed to attract attention without lowering themselves by appearing too commercial. Today with the rising cost of paid advertising and fierce competition, all types of businesses are turning more and more to nonpaid methods.

Perhaps the most appealing benefit of publicizing your business is how it generates customers. By carefully cultivating promotional activities, you can attract customers at a much lower cost than by concentrating on paid advertising alone, and since repeat business is the secret to success in just about any enterprise, the less spent to attract customers in the first place makes good sense and higher profits.

### Making sure customers think of you

Your overall goal with any promotional activity is to get the public's attention in a positive way, create good will, and gain support and acceptance. The old adage "no news is good news" doesn't apply in your case. You want your business in the public eye, so don't be shy. Promote and promote often. The down side of promotion and publicity is that it's more difficult to control than paid advertising.

While you have complete control over space size and content with paid ads, a journalist makes all decisions about the editorial content of his or her paper. And unlike paid ads which generate a quick but fleeting buck, regular publicity is more like quietly making deposits into a savings account. It's the difference between taking straight aim at the bull's-eye and casting your net into the water. If sited properly, paying to advertise makes a direct hit on your target

*"We are a very locally-oriented paper and rarely print mass-mailed releases."*

David Ruble, Managing Editor
**The Charles City Press**
Charles City, Iowa

market, albeit an expensive one. On the other hand, promotion and publicity is more like seining; you're not sure how many you'll bring up with each cast, but throwing out the net enough times in the right spots will surely produce a bountiful catch.

Consistently repeating your message to potential customers eventually pays off when they're ready to buy, and each promotional exercise you plan and carry out reinforces your message. Customers must know who you are and what you can do for them.

Repeating publicity through several activities over time allows your message to penetrate the gray matter and to begin drawing interest and paying dividends of public confidence. By reinforcing the image you want to project and boosting your credibility, news releases are an investment in the long-range success of your business. With a little analysis, promoting with news releases can tell you a lot about other low-cost promotional activities to try and where to spend ad dollars for the best return. Patience here ceases to be a virtue and becomes an absolute necessity. The expectations of an immediate return on every investment can dilute effectiveness if you don't allow your plan time to work. Develop your news release plan; then have the patience to see it through. Impact is built over time, not overnight.

Business promotion is a state of mind. It's developing your own fine-tuned radar that's always scanning the horizon, ever alert, picking up signals of opportunity. It's preparing yourself to not only recognize an opening, but to step in when the time is right. You must first develop your radar and then develop a plan

*"All small towns have ties to larger towns. It is the larger town that provides many of the goods and services not available in the rural areas. If a business in a large city recognizes that connection to the surrounding rural area, and incorporates that knowledge into press releases, then that business will be able to get free 'advertising' in the home town paper 50 or 60 miles away and attract more customers from other areas who are making the trek to the city anyway."*

Ralph B. Davis III, Editor
*The Jackson County Sun*
McKee, Kentucky

of action that places you in the best position to jump on the opportunities when they come along.

During Desert Storm, patriotism soared into the ionosphere, and the American people screamed for symbols and souvenirs as a way to show their support. Many small business people redirected their efforts to take advantage of the renewed spirit, quickly cranking out items of clothing, bumper stickers, games, and books to meet the demand. One firm in Killeen, TX offered a personalized bracelet for $7.95 engraved with the name of the military man or woman of your choice serving in the Gulf along with the words "Operation Desert Shield." Inscribed on the underside were the words "until you return." The diMarcos of San Jose, California put together a Letters To The Troops Stationery Kit priced at $4.50.

These and dozens of other businesses saw what was coming when Iraq invaded Kuwait and moved to meet the public's rising demand to be part of the crisis. The memento makers saw a need and responded to fill it at exactly the right time -- and made sure to alert the media.

Begin by thinking of your business activities as they might relate to what's going on in your community. Later, as your abilities to relate sharpen, expand your thinking to the state, the U.S., and even the world. Watch for events to use in your favor. It's always easy to get publicity by being "the first," but to be first you must know in advance the direction in which your target market is headed, and what they will want when they get there.

*"Far too many 'news' releases are almost out-and-out advertising copy. 'News' should be <u>news</u>!"*

A. J. Pinder, Publisher
***Grinnell Herald-Register***
Grinnell, Iowa

For example, Kennesaw, GA, a quiet little town just north of Atlanta, was never a den of criminal activity, but town leaders recognized a growing national trend in 1982, and moved to become the first community in the country to pass a law requiring all heads of households to own and maintain a firearm. The action produced a flurry of publicity and thrust Kennesaw into the national spotlight. Ten years after all the jokes about gun-totin' rednecks have died down, town leaders continue to report a declining crime rate. Publicity creates a powerful public image, and in Kennesaw's case, that image is one of no nonsense when it comes to the criminal element. Apparently the crooks got the message. The law and subsequent publicity has done precisely what was intended.

One word of caution about being first: Make sure any unexplored territory doesn't conceal trap doors through which everything you've worked so hard for may fall.

## The right image

While news release publicity accounts for but one slice of the nonpaid promotional pie, it's certainly the most important because of its positive impact on the success of other activities you choose, since you'll naturally want to publicize each one. And since most small business operators are perpetually strapped for cash, news releases provide an excellent vehicle to begin promoting your business. Besides, whether you're just planning a new business or are well on your way, the prospects of so-called 'free advertising' should make your mouth water. Planning a news

*"We rarely, if ever, run a news release unedited or as is. I really only use news releases as news tips. And it's going to have to be something that affects, or is of interest to, our local readers. Most of the releases are pretty self-serving and require more work, fleshing this out -- if they're usable."*

Mike Stepanovich,
Business Editor
***The Bakersfield Californian***
Bakersfield, California

release campaign forces you to think about your target market, the image you want the public to see, and your company's philosophy, the very cornerstone on which to build a sound marketing plan.

Taking a good hard look at your organization and its mission is fundamental when developing a news release campaign just as it is when formulating the overall marketing strategy. Your business reflects the personalities of the principles. If you are the sole proprietor, your enterprise is an extension of yourself and carries your brand all over it. Is this the image you want the public to see?

The character of a partnership becomes a mix of each individual personality. Avoid disputes later by agreeing on your business image -- along with

everything else -- before you ever commit to working together. Likewise, a corporation without a well-defined and firmly ingrained public image suffers if everyone in the corporation presents a different face when dealing with customers.

Truly great organizations go beyond just having an image to a higher, more cerebral place wherein leaders with vision reside. Vision gives ordinary working men and women the power to make a difference. Vision is the glue that holds the parts together and the spirit that empowers the whole organization not only to attain an extraordinary level of success, but to excel at that level -- the kind of proficiency that leaves the competition shocked and bewildered.

Vision allows organizations to pursue extremely high principles and pushes companies to set unbelievable goals and reach them. Companies with vision create an atmosphere in which employees experience a sense of purpose about their work, where they are freely chartered to affect customer satisfaction and thus possess an intense feeling of responsibility for it. And they back up those feelings with action from the gut. Vision is not something that just happens to giants like Wal-Mart, Home Depot, and Microsoft -- *how do you think they got to be giants*? They had vision as pups and, though individual leaders may change, the mindset instilled in the beginning keeps working.

Start planning your news release campaign by thinking about your business image. Perhaps you've not given much thought to having a business image, much less to using it as a promotional tool. That image stuff is some high-dollar glitz and shine manufactured by Madison Avenue types -- all hype and no substance -- in order to stick it to the American consumer in a nice way. True, many businesses operate under a veil of deceit, a posture by no means limited to small-time charlatans.

Some of America's giants have the corporate conscience of a snake-oil salesman, yet for years have spoon-fed the American public massive doses of expensive advertising proclaiming otherwise. In 1819 President Thomas Jefferson wrote "advertisements contained the only truths to be relied on in a newspaper."[1] Times have certainly changed. We've been bombarded by so many false claims that virtually all paid advertising now passes without so much as a casual notice. Paying good money to tell a lie about what your customers can expect just does not make good sense, though many routinely rely on the practice. When advertisers all make the same product claims, intelligent buyers have nothing to go on except reputation. Create demand by building a good reputation. If your products and services are of good value and you see to it that the customer succeeds, then your own success will naturally follow.

Mannerisms, speech, and general attitude combine to create your business personality and the image your employees and customers have of you. *True story*: A new deli opened in a nearby strip center. It looked appealing from the street so my husband and I decided to try it out. It was 11:45 on a work day in a business district of a major metropolitan suburb. When we walked in we noticed that, other than the two unhurried older gentlemen behind the counter, the place was dark and empty. Just then one of the men reached over and flipped on the lights. It's almost noon, I thought, a little late to just be opening a lunch counter. My husband nodded, they didn't, we took our seats, ordered, ate, paid, and left. During the entire 25 minutes, only one other person came in to eat.

What's your impression of the new eatery? I can remember absolutely nothing about the quality of my sandwich. The food was not what got my attention. To us, the experience completely defied the image projected by the attractive window dressing that

*"The newspaper sees itself as a community servant, so it sees those who demand services . . . without ever giving back as ungrateful and selfish."*

Rhonda Vines, News Editor
***Haralson-Gateway Beacon***
Bremen, Georgia

pulled us inside. I wound up feeling almost as if they didn't want us there. Was the owner stingy or strapped for cash? What else could explain his failure to turn the lights on *before* we walked in? Do you suppose the owner resented our dirty plates because of the impact on his water bill? I suspect he was *in business to make money*, an all-too-common miscalculation, but a most deliberate and diligently practiced philosophy. That sort of thinking cuts out the key ingredient -- customers. Without customers there is eventually no business in which to be. Serving customers is all that matters. The deli might still be building sandwiches for the lunch crowd had it adopted a more palatable business philosophy toward its bread and butter.

Be in business *to give customers excellent product quality and service at a price that will make money*. The way you conduct your business influences the way people think of you. Create the right illusion. If your head is in the right place, everything else becomes exceedingly less complicated.

We, the consumers, once obediently bought all the same inferior mass-produced goods which we used up and threw away. Not any more. Spendable income is down, the landfills are full, and we now demand quality goods that last longer and the respect a value-oriented shopper deserves. We will no longer be taken for granted. We expect service and will pay extra for it. We'll go out of our way to do business with someone we know won't burn us if something goes wrong after the sale, someone we have come to believe in. What was it that made us feel we could trust them? Just when did we start believing?

Don't the places you feel the best about project the same image through their marketing efforts that you feel and see when you actually go into the store to buy?

The business which claims to be "the helpful store" does not live up to its image when you can't find a salesperson who knows anything. The department store that expands and remodels and then proudly boasts "we're changing to serve you better" does nothing to improve public opinion when customers encounter the same old attitudes. If you adopt "the friendly store" as your slogan, then that's your promise and the impression your customers must take away. If customers experience neutral or unfriendly employees, your projected image doesn't match behavior and you're guilty of deception for not living up to your promise.

Why do some operations treat us as we deserve to be treated only after we become a problem? It simply comes down to how those charged with projecting and protecting "the image" are trained. Create an image you can live with, then decide what you want to accomplish consistent with your image. Unfortunately far too few enterprises have a well-defined image. Those that do have usually also departed from what is considered a normal level of performance, and for their efforts can claim throngs of devoted customers. It all begins with your perceived business image.

Perceptions are real. As humans, what we believe to be true is. In a 1991 survey conducted by *Working Woman* magazine, readers believed the greatest incidence of unethical behavior occurs in government followed by sales, law, media, finance, medicine, banking, and manufacturing. Your position on that list right behind Uncle Sam might indicate just how much guilt by association you will have to overcome. If your particular business carries a general stigma anyway, like "contractors never show up when promised" or "all truck drivers think they own the road," your preconceived image may be quite a formidable obstacle.

As customers, especially when it's our first encounter, one bad experience with a business can be enough to convince us to shop elsewhere. We perceive them to be unworthy, therefore they are. It makes no difference how others may feel. Our impressions are the only ones that count and if we believe it, it's real. Conversely, if we believe a business to be honest and fair, then they are, and we are very reluctant to be persuaded otherwise. This is what consistently good experiences as a customer, and promotional activities that parallel those experiences, will do for you. It sets an image in the mind of the customer that shall not be shaken. Since you can't put a dollar value on a good reputation, many business people feel it's an insignificant commodity. But thinking back to their own last substantial purchase during financially tough times should be enough to convince them otherwise; when consumers part with tight money, they spend it where they feel the most comfortable.

The message here is clear: Create an image you can and will live up to, then seize every opportunity to tell the world about it. Establish an identity you believe in and repeat it over and over in your promotional

*"Ads disguised as news releases are 'round-filed' immediately. Our readers are too smart for that, and so are we."*

Terry O'Connor,
Managing Editor
***Boone County Recorder***
Florence, Kentucky

activities. Concentrate news releases on selling your good name rather than products or services. If you are just starting out and no one's ever heard of you, create an identity with news releases, reinforce and build on it by continually repeating your message, then take advantage of *the demand you create* with paid advertising later.

Sometimes changes in business require delicate handling in the media to avoid or minimize bad publicity. Perhaps at no other time do the benefits of a public relations campaign that mirrors a good reputation pay off than when faced with an undesirable situation that comes to the attention of the public. If you keep your customers in mind, admit your mistakes, and show a unwavering sense of social responsibility by developing a tangible plan to fix the problem -- and do what you say -- you unload the gun of any detractor before they can cock the hammer.

Ethics in business is something we've been hearing and reading a lot about lately, though it seems to be coming mostly from people on the outside looking in -- writers and consultants. Preachy advice to live by the Golden Rule during the work day may come across as naive theory, but following your conscience and consistently doing the right thing projects an image customers appreciate, and goes along way toward giving you the benefit of the doubt in complicated or delicate situations.

Should a crisis occur, make a special effort to contact major customers to let them know how you plan to rectify the situation, and reassure them by outlining the action you've taken to see it never happens again. Advanced planning means you are ready should adverse conditions affect your business. Neglecting to plan leaves no other option but to take a reactionary position. It's better to take aim than to shoot from the hip. If you've consistently done right by your customers, and reminded them of it at every opportunity, you should come out of any unpleasantness with little or no lasting negative impact on your public image.

## Watch for trends

Once you have looked at your organization and its image, the next step is to begin looking for trends. Trends move us, make us think, and influence our opinions and behavior. Since we learn about trends largely through the media, then it would be more accurate to say the *latest information* about trends impacts our feelings and decision making. Public interest (trend drivers) dictates what a newspaper editor chooses to publish, and those interests are constantly in a state of flux.

Five major trends affect American opinions and behavior right now. Their order of importance -- how most people would rank them on any given day -- can change according to daily events and regional conditions. During the research and writing of this book, the poor state of the national economy was constantly in the news and could be listed as the number one trend -- the general topic of most interest, concern, and conversation for huge numbers of people. Tomorrow or next week any one of the other

## Major Trends

| Economy | Drugs/Crime | Health/AIDS | Environment | Family |
|---|---|---|---|---|
| higher crime rate | loss of jobs | fear | loss of jobs | drugs/crime |
| health coverage | fear | greater awareness | recycling | moms work |
| loss of jobs | child abuse | medical breakthroughs | health problems | moral code |
| less spending | deteriorating family | control of treatment | childrens' future | aging parents |
| fear | welfare reform | cost of care | hazardous waste | |
| moms work | | moral code | | |
| welfare reform | | | | |

**This brief list shows how developments in one trend spill over into others. Add your market's specific concerns.**

major trends -- drugs and crime, health and AIDS, the environment, or the changing family could be considered number one.

National trends intertwine in a cause and effect relationship. For example, drugs and crime are often blamed on a sagging economy, and health problems are considered by many the consequence of exposure to an unsafe environment. Anyone from New Hampshire and New Mexico could meet for the first time and freely discuss each of today's major trends but, depending on their own set of circumstances, it's likely opinions may differ slightly on which trend most influences their own day-to-day lives. At the local level, trends become very specific and pockets of real change begin to take place, thus trend shifts develop; one aspect of a trend becomes less important as a new one emerges, and like tossing a rock into a pond, major trend shifts radiate up and out to the national level.

By knowing the trends, watching their movement, and staying in touch with how your market feels about them, you can plan how to address any particular one to your best advantage in a news release. Timely releases make the most impact because they deal with subjects of interest *now* and greatly increase you chances of getting into print.

Let's assume for a minute that an area in your community discovered to be a toxic waste dump has captured the headlines lately. What's the major trend? The environment. What's happening? Many families are being temporarily moved and the origins of serious illnesses suddenly no longer seem so mysterious. Crews are working to remove the waste material and clean up the soil and ground water.

How in the world can you relate that to your small gift shop or consulting business to get publicity? Should you even try? After all, these are your neighbors, and you wouldn't think of capitalizing on their misfortune. Relax. You are not making out at someone else's expense. Quite the contrary. You have identified an opportunity to make a difference. By taking correct and responsible action, and letting the public know about it, you become part of the solution.

Start a recycling program, and write a news release. Businesses everywhere are beginning to recycle and making a point of letting customers know. We now carry groceries home in shopping bags made of recycled paper or plastic. How do we know that? It's stamped in big letters on every bag. Do we believe it's true? It better be. The last thing you want to do is tell the public one thing and do another. Of course, it's not necessary to wait for a toxic waste dump to be uncovered to start recycling. I mention it only as a

*"I have long felt that saturation mailings of releases that were almost certainly doomed from the outset is a major economic problem and a burden on our postal system."*

William M. Hays
Editor & Publisher
***Washington County News***
Washington, Kansas

sensational example of community happenings in which you may find an opportunity for a plug in the local paper. Hometown journalists look for local impact of national trends. Since recycling is "trendy" and viewed as the socially responsible thing to do, it's a lot more likely to receive a few lines in the local newspaper than a release promoting a new widget.

Too small? Ok, just how much impact can one paper shuffler working out of a spare bedroom part time make? Issue a challenge to others. See how many similar small timers you can get to pitch in together for "good old Mother Earth." For incentive, promise to include them in the news release. To reap the benefits, sometimes you have to share the spotlight. Use your imagination. Write an initial release to issue the challenge then send out others as progress reports. Set a goal. Submit a celebration photo of participants when the goal is met. The possibilities for this sort of indirect, noncommercial business *news* are practically endless and the only kind that get published. Find a trend, parallel a business activity, and write a news release about it.

The day after the Braves clinched the National League pennant in 1991, a tiny Atlanta graphics design firm hand-delivered championship T-shirts in red gift bags to all of its clients. The gesture received nine lines in the Business Section of *The Atlanta Constitution*. The Braves' title quest mesmerized fans for weeks. Even people professing no great love for the sport could not be torn from their TV sets during the race for the division and league championships. The entire region was bonkers with excitement. The firm's owner, Joel Sarrett,

*"A store owner should not expect any newspaper to give free news space when he refuses to advertise."*

Ronald C. Slechta, Publisher
*The Kalena News*
Kalena, Iowa

recognized intense public interest and created a business activity that paralleled that interest. He delighted customers with the hottest item in town and gave the editor of the morning edition something of interest to readers. Bingo.

The closer you resemble the way your customers see themselves, the more sales you'll make. If your customers perceive that you share their same values, they'll favor you over the competition. Go where your customers go, do what they do, and develop news releases with their interests in mind.

What is your reason for being in business? Can you successfully project that motivation into a believable image you can and will live up to? If you are just trying to get people in the door six days a week to pay the bills, it will show, and customers will be left with little motivation to return. Perhaps you are not yet established. You can develop an image with news releases and other promotional activities, then benefit from the mindset created as you grow. Develop an image that carries through everything you do from business cards now to TV commercials later. Create an image with publicity, then put it to work for profits.

A good way to begin creating a business image is by thinking about what is important to you personally and to your organization. Start by answering the following questions.

- What are your strengths?
- What are your weaknesses?
- What exactly is affecting your bottom line, good

or bad? (When looking to place blame here, remember management is responsible for 85% of all business problems in America. Look at yourself first.)

• Are earnings where they should be?  If not, why?

• What improvements can you make and how will you do it?

• Is quality what it should be?

• Is the price right?

• Have you instilled the company goals in your employees so that they work as a team toward reaching them?

• Are you a good citizen?

• What do you do for your community?

• How have you changed from a year ago?

• Five years ago?

• Have attitudes changed? How? Why?

• What are incoming phone calls and mail telling you about the attitudes of your suppliers and customers?

• Where do you want to be in a year?

• In five?

• What do you want then?

Your answers to these questions may be surprising. Many times it isn't easy to identify marketing problems, and perhaps you'll uncover some of which you were not previously aware. By thinking creatively, maybe a solution to a problem that's puzzled you for some time will suddenly become clear. Besides these benefits, you should get a pretty good idea of what your employees and the public think of you, and make a conscientious effort to change what you don't like. Wherever you perceive a weakness to be tarnishing your image, fix the problem and then let the public know about what you have done.

Suppose you're known for prices that are "too high." If customers can get comparable product quality cheaper elsewhere, you've got a problem. On the other hand, if you pay a great deal of attention to detail when selecting each product and thus returns for poor quality are nonexistent, potential customers may be more willing to part with the extra money -- that is, if they know why. But submitting a news release about just how persnickety you are when it comes to product quality probably won't work. You must use a more indirect approach. Try, for instance, a naturally humorous release about picky people in general. Since we all know one or two, readers will be able to relate to the familiar idiosyncrasy. The trend in this example could be the disappearance of good, old fashioned craftsmanship, not a banner issue but a very common complaint and no less genuine. Cite some examples, including your own quirk, to achieve the free exposure you desire.

If you take nothing else from this chapter, remember three things about marketing in general and publicity and promotion in particular -- image, image, image. Sounds simple, but many large corporations have lousy ones and do nothing to change until forced by the competition. Even then, some take reactionary measures that punish their customers more than before. Many small business people so completely absorb themselves with the job at hand they never stop to think about their image. You should. Remember, developing an image you can and will live up to is fundamental to success, not a fringe benefit of it. Knowing your target market and exercising a good sense of timing are key to successful promotion, and it's imperative you know what that market is before you can know how to reach it. As obvious as this sounds, I must say it because, like my friend Tom who didn't have a complete grasp of what business he was in, many small business hopefuls think they know who their potential customers are, yet they don't know, or they once knew but have forgotten. Don't be so impatient to get started that you later find yourself going the wrong way. News releases can't help a misdirected endeavor.

One final note: Publicity begets publicity. Be sure to include in your marketing plan how you'll handle all the new customers.

## Chapter Key Points

• Think about what business you are in and what image you want to convey.
• Remember who your customers are and how you will reach them.
• Pay attention to trend movements affecting your target market.
• Develop ideas for publicity by paralleling business activities to trends.
• Write it all down in a workable plan.

# 3

# Working With Editors

- **The maddening media**
- **Understanding the species**
- **Media relations**
- **Become the expert**
- **Handling negative publicity**
- **News vs. Ads**
- **What is 'News Value'?**
- **No overwritten news full of holes, please**
- **First impressions**
- **Photos & illustrations**
- **Follow-up & deadlines**

No matter which print media you intend to target for your news releases, the one person standing squarely between you and the publicity you need and want is a journalist. I cannot overemphasize your need to understand what makes him or her tick. Read the following carefully. It's the complete formula.

*To get your business activities in print, your material must only impact the editor in charge of the publication you want to carry your message. Period.*

That's the one and only requirement. No fine print. No hidden add-ons. That's it. Forget crafting words designed to appeal to your target market. Forget any suggestion that it's a completely incalculable gamble -

*"My dream news release is clearly written, typed double-spaced, has a local angle or focus, is concise, arrives on time, and gives me a contact name and telephone number."*

Tina M. Kunkler, Editor
*LaRue County Herald News*
Hodgenville, Kentucky

- mail out a boxcar load of them and pray. As your promotional "significant other," the more you know about the editor and the role he plays, the better your chances of getting published.

### The maddening media

The media are constantly on the lookout for material with fresh new angles -- for *change* -- in our ever-changing world. Newspapers, magazines, and trade journals are businesses too, and they are as intent upon giving their customers what they want as you are. Of course, regularly delivering all that useful and entertaining information has never directly generated a single dime. The money maker is a newspaper's ability to attract readers, which in turn attracts advertisers with money to buy space. The more readership, the higher the rate they can charge advertisers.

Paid advertising is the major source of revenue for the overwhelming majority of American newspapers, and though news and ads are practically as separate as church and state, the fact remains that without advertising revenue to pay the bills, news would be either a lot more expensive or nonexistent as we know it.

Big city newspapers must fill thousands of column inches of news space with pertinent, up-to-date material about unusual people and events every single day. Even the biggest and best can't do it alone. Blessed with a wealth of resources and scores of news writers, large dailies still rely on unsolicited news

*"As a specialized publication, the AJT is very much concerned with whether releases are relevant to our particular audience. If I were to list my biggest complaint with those who submit material, it is that they so often clearly haven't looked at our publication to see what kind of material we publish."*

Fran Rothbard, Managing Editor
***Atlanta Jewish Times***
Atlanta, Georgia

releases, or at least their inspiration, to help plug the gap between the amount of material the staff can dig up and the amount of space that must be filled.

Large operations employ many specialized editors who begin their day assigning stories to dozens of beat reporters and photographers. While the reporters and photographers are out gathering facts and freezing events on film, editors pour over wire service stories, go through stacks of mail, and feed all suitable material to a copy editor who makes sure that stories conform to the publication's style. In the meantime, editors attend meetings, consult with staff artists for appropriate illustrations, and sweat out pulling it all together by deadline. Big city editors spend their lives under a permanent strain to beat the competition with timely, interesting, well-written material by the next press run.

On the other end of the spectrum, small-town community newspapers with but a single editor usually face less competitive pressure and can claim far fewer resources, but still must fill a chunk of space left over after placing all staff-generated articles. Far removed from the pressure-cooker newsrooms of big city dailies, the small town editor has his or her own set of problems. This "jack-of-all-trades" many times also plays the role of publisher and must not only decide what news to include in each issue, but sell advertising and manage the business end of things. He often writes a column, fills in as staff photographer when needed, and even has a hand in laying out the paper and pasting it up. Keenly and thoroughly scrutinized front to back, small town newspapers devote their entire news holes to local happenings.

*"As tight as our newshole is, most releases are dumped unless there is a direct application to our circulation area."*

William C. Baker, Editor
***The Clinton Herald***
Clinton, Iowa

Hometown readers are quick to note errors and slow to forget them. For the person selling the ads and deciding what is news, ticklish situations sometimes arise when major advertisers begin to believe they have paid for the right to direct the paper's editorial content. The editor's free hand at publishing all the news without fear of financial reprisal rests first with how well his personal integrity holds up under pressure, and second, with his ability to educate the business community about sound newspaper publishing principles.

*The Blackshear Times*, a rural weekly serving Blackshear, GA, sums up the condition of all small town newspapers in it's slogan: *Liked by many, cussed by some, read by them all*.

Somewhere in between large daily newspapers and small circulation community weeklies falls an endless number of magazine, trade, and professional journal editors. In recent years mass-appeal magazines have given way to more specialized publications targeting narrow segments of the population with a particular interest.

Trade publications serve those within a specific occupation or industry. Professional journals cater to specific disciplines like engineering or nursing. In this age of specialization, publications have emerged to fill the need for even more specialized information, confining coverage to topics of interest only to civil engineers, for example, or just emergency room nurses. Editors of these publications share the stress of deadlines and the necessity to continually feed their hungry readers with new and interesting material, and they depend on news releases to do it. Your target market likely includes many individuals with varying interests and occupations, but as a news release writer, rather than think about your market, instead you must appeal solely to the readership of the publication.

News publications serve readers according to either a specific interest or a geographic area. Beyond that it's impossible to cite standardizations in organization. No two are exactly alike. Local conditions, financial position, and degree of journalistic expertise dictate differences in operation.

The publisher shoulders overall responsibility as the outright owner of the newspaper or as an employee answering to the owner. He or she sets editorial policy and manages the financial side of the house. The editor directs the news staff within policies set forth by the publisher. The managing editor handles the day-to-day editorial activities, coordinating the work of departmental editors and other staffers, and is first to gnaw fingernails to the quick as a deadline approaches. Departmental editors (news editor, business editor, etc.) coordinate the work of staff writers and photographers and report to the managing editor. The organization just described generally can be found at a large to mid-size newspaper, but for small operations the org chart usually stops at the editor. Smaller papers sometimes do enough business to support a managing editor with a small staff, or perhaps a news editor with an even smaller staff.

The media need you as much as you need them. Though editors may use only one in every 10 releases

*"We don't have time to [suggest improvements]. However, we do tell them why the release isn't newsworthy."*

Mike Patrick, Managing Editor
***Arizona Daily Sun***
Flagstaff, Arizona

received, survey results show unsolicited news releases occupy 19% of editorial space. And it's not at all unusual for the people you read about to have actually written the articles. Businesses receive publicity because they actively pursue opportunities for it. Think of it as a bartering arrangement; editors have empty space to fill, and you have a perspective on business uniquely yours to offer in trade.

## Understanding the species

Since editors exercise absolute control over any quest for publicity, you should know as much about them as possible. Studies reveal reporters tend to be sophisticated, young, white males with liberal leanings, though women and minorities have begun entering the field in large numbers in recent years.[2]

Whether it's a trait inherently present in individuals most at home in the occupation or as a result of it, journalists are a little crazy. As noted American foreign correspondent H.R. Knickerbocker once observed, journalists are the only humans on earth that want to get in a place from which literally hundreds of thousands are trying desperately to flee.[3]

Journalists in general, especially those in broadcast media, are not a popular lot with the public. They nose around where they are not wanted and ask stupid, embarrassing questions. To decent folks, their insensitivity to the obvious pain of others borders on barbarism; they feed on smut and indecency with a sharklike frenzy, and ignorantly portray American free enterprise as evil. (Someone once said all newspaper editorial writers ever do is come down from the hills after the battle is over and shoot the wounded.4)

An extreme and stereotypical picture, true. So is the widely held view by journalists that business executives forsake everything for the bottom line, even "selling their own grandmother" if it means another nickel of profit. Business executives can smile and look you straight in the eye while lying. They will deny rumored plans to close the plant one week and throw lifelong employees out into the streets the next.

Look beyond common biases and avoid stereotypical behavior and attitudes if you wish to develop a mutually beneficial relationship with media professionals.

We have anointed journalists as our leaders. We allow them a strong hand in creating our mindset by willingly inviting them into our homes to freely express whatever ideas and information they believe to be important. We encourage their activities with our subscriptions and advertising. Publications prosper in direct proportion to the public's perception of how well they do their job. Media "gatekeepers" shoulder ultimate responsibility for deciding what information reaches the public, and it's not so unusual for decisions to be based on their own values and tastes rather than the actual importance of the material. And since different stories appeal to different editors, studying the type and style of articles appearing in the print medium you wish to target will tell you a great deal about the editor with whom you will be dealing.

*"Before submitting news releases, people should consider whether or not the subject matter is really news, or whether they need to be be contacting a sales representative at the target publication."*

Rick Thomason, Editor
***The Dothan Progress***
Dothan, Alabama

Journalists deal with and must be able to talk to all types of people in pursuit of the facts, but the pressures of deadlines and competing publications complicates matters. Whether by nature or by training or both, journalists are suspicious and skeptical. Moreover, many literally dodge bullets to get as close to the story as possible.

It is understandable then why news reporters aren't easily impressed and can appear distant. It is the compulsive drive for objectivity -- disinterest, detachment, noninvolvement -- which creates barriers, sometimes prompting their treatment of news sources as disposable objects to use up and discard.

No matter how hot the news, a journalist is bound by professional ethics to approach it coldly and impersonally. Editors want the facts of the story, not the writer's personal or emotional impressions. The best news writers learn to string facts together in a way that is fresh yet strictly accurate.

The harried journalist jockeys to be first to print an interesting story with more in-depth details, conduct a better interview by digging out crucial information, write well enough to draw the reader in, inform or entertain, so he or she can in turn sell more papers, all on a very rapid and rigid schedule. Whatever you can do to ease the process will help your cause. In this age of information, reporters are charged with observing, listening, questioning and, most importantly, understanding complex subjects and events so they can impartially pass on the most vital facts with lightning speed to a demanding public.

*"We don't run free ads on products and services posing as news."*

Larry Grooms, Editor-in-Chief
*Antelope Valley Press*
Palmdale, California

Required aptitude for a journalist includes perceiving, comprehending, and interpreting bits of information, then pulling them all together in news writing style. He or she has a good general knowledge of history, economics, government, politics, science, law, and at least a passing acquaintance with a foreign language or two. Additionally, journalists must keep up with current events and write simply and naturally about them.

They are expected to know the difference between the IRA claiming responsibility for acts of violence in the United Kingdom and the IRA many Americans expect to supplement their retirement income, and use the terms in the correct context. They are expected to recognize when new information is really news. Still, the mound of mail and faxes each day suggests only the most learned and aggressive news professionals can spot the really important pieces correctly portraying newsworthy developments.

An editor decides to publish your piece based on whether it meets the changing demands of his readers, not because it serves your need for publicity. Media coverage happens sometimes against long odds, but those who succeed have developed the ability to anticipate, recognize, and respond to subtle changes in public concern. The editor responds when he opens your piece of mail describing a person, event, or activity at just the precise point of change where he perceives his readers' interest to be.

While firing off a news release with the same pinpoint accuracy as a stealth bomber over Bagdad may sound like a tall order, developing material editors consider timely that also serves your own self-interests is not at all difficult if you learn to think about your business activities the right way.

## Media relations

Submitting good news releases to the same publication on a regular schedule does more than just increase your chances of one being published. Consistently newsworthy material helps establish a rapport with the editor that each subsequent release nurtures.

Of the unsolicited news releases received each day, the editor must decide which ones, if any, suit his or her readers, and of those, which ones can be trusted to be truthful. When confronted with material from an unfamiliar firm, the editor must judge the content and decide if he can risk the chance of misleading the readers. After receiving several from the same source, he naturally begins to feel less tentative.

Your planned schedule of newsworthy releases will build credibility for news value with the editor, and he will begin to recognize your envelop and look forward to seeing what you have to offer.

Contributing journalists were twice as likely to base their decision about running a particular news release on their familiarity with the reputation of the submitting person or organization. A full 33 percent said their choice was very often based on previous knowledge, while another 32 percent said familiarity was sometimes the deciding factor.

*"I do occasionally use news releases that have no direct connection to our community, but only as optional 'filler' material."*

Tina M. Kunkler, Editor
*LaRue County Herald News*
Hodgenville, Kentucky

You want to cultivate good "press relations." That means exercising common sense when dealing with newspaper professionals. Be courteous, be considerate, and above all, be open and honest. Remember the editor knows you're trying to get a free plug. Dropping names or throwing your weight around won't get you anywhere. Leaning on friends in the business to run a particular story begs for strained relations, but it's ok to ask them to read your material and make suggestions for improvement. If any is offered, by all means accept it gratefully.

Publicity is manipulative when the information submitted is intentionally false or misleading. Any attempt to deceive the public through the media is a time bomb that will eventually go off to the discredit of the submitter and to the detriment of the publication that prints it. A good reputation is easier to gain than to regain. Just as a mistreated customer will likely never return, it's highly improbable that a scorched editor will consider future releases for a long, long time.

Legitimate news publications fiercely guard their reputation. Within the limits of time and budget, editors strive to confirm a source's reliability and the accuracy and perceived news value of the information. Unfortunately when exaggerations, distortions, or outright misrepresentations do slip by, both the editor and the publication lose credibility and, in severe cases, readers and advertisers go elsewhere. Your goal is to take advantage of opportunities for publicity, not to exploit the journalist and the medium for which he works.

Establish yourself as a credible contributor. Remember, an important step toward gaining the public's trust is gaining the trust of an editor. One of the biggest hurdles to getting the publicity you want will evaporate simply by establishing a consistent pattern of honesty and straightforwardness. The rewards for credibility and the patience to establish it in the long run will far outweigh any short-lived gains you may grab from one deceptive maneuver.

The public demands information about new products and production methods, new services and benefits, and new techniques and technologies. Consider for a minute how different our lives would be if all the Steve Jobs in this country had no other outlet than paid advertising to tell the world about their revolutionary new ideas. Computers would still be agonizingly unfriendly and found only in large corporations able to afford them. Jobs would still be sitting in his parent's garage with his nifty little device called a "microcomputer" (which launched Apple), and the author would be writing all of this on a typewriter. The greatest invention of the 20th century may not have gotten off the ground.

Publicity drives the economy and the public's demand for *newer*, *better*, *easier* drives the media. This would not be America without it. Our free-market economy thrives on business promotion and publicity. New products and production methods, new services and benefits, and new techniques and technologies is news just as much as crime or tax legislation. However most small businesses will never invent anything so new as to be previously nonexistent. Commonly advised though badly off the mark, businesses should forget releases promoting products and services altogether. Editors see them as advertising, and in the trash they go. You don't need the greatest invention of the 21st Century; your business activities can become news if you learn to think about them from a "news" perspective.

## Become the expert

Good media relations can contribute to the success of your company. As a natural development of positive publicity over time, you'll become recognized as a community leader and an expert in your field, and editors are likely to begin calling on you for insight and interpretation as change generates new information regarding your industry. You may remember the statement "publicity begets publicity" at the end of the previous chapter. Media exposure tends to elevate one to a position of "expert," thus drawing more media exposure.

To give meaning, relevance, and perspective to new information, good reporters include in their stories comments by recognized leaders -- those known to be authorities on a subject largely because of prior media exposure. The input of experts on how new information fits into what's happened in the past and how it will influence the future helps readers understand the issues and make better decisions.

Expert news sources are in such demand by the media that one company has developed a nationwide

*"A wise old newspaper publisher once told me, 'Son, if you give it away, you sure can't sell it.' His point was that if a news release is really advertising a business, new product, etc., make those who benefit pay for the space they want in the newspaper. We are inundated with so-called news releases that are advertising. As a result, very few make it past my waste paper basket."*

Randy Sunderland,
Managing Editor
***Delta County Independent***
Delta, Colorado

directory. Broadcast Interview Source of Washington, DC recently released its 11th Edition *Yearbook of Experts, Authorities & Spokespersons*, and the company claims among its subscribers respected news organizations such as CNN, ***The Washington Post***, and ***USA Today***.

The directory indexes expert sources by topic, zip code, and alphabetically, and those listed have paid to be included. Each individual or organization advertises why they qualify allowing the media to pick and choose the best candidate for the story angle. For more information write to Mitchell P. Davis, Editor, 2233 Wisconsin Ave. NW, Washington, DC 20007-4104, or call 800-955-0311 (202-333-4904 in the DC area).

The point is exposure in the press validates legitimacy. Repeat coverage strengthens your claim, therefore positioning yourself as *the* expert in your field guarantees future publicity. Of course publicity heightens "name recognition" and ultimately produces more customers for your business. Again, be prepared to handle them.

Unfortunately some so-called news makers achieve unmerited status merely by being accessible to the press. Perhaps your competition comes to mind. It's a good bet the regular attention he or she receives in the newspaper, at least in part, can be attributed to a sustained period of good relations with the media. His or her lofty position and bank account will only continue to grow unless you make an effort to get your share of the headlines.

Once you have established a reputation for credibility with news releases, you may want to suggest an interview. When requesting an interview, state your purpose and the benefits the editor will receive up front. Remember, to get an interview you will have to have something the editor believes will be of interest to his readers. It'll be a very short meeting if you bait an editor and then don't deliver, and your last for a very long time no matter how good the information you have for him next month.

Since editors and reporters live and die by deadlines, it is essential to return phone calls and handle requests promptly. If you promise something, deliver. If they need something, make sure you get it to them on time.

Reporters are human too, and subject to the same prejudices as other people. If you feel a face-to-face interview may place you at a disadvantage because of a perceived prejudice, suggest a telephone interview. Common factors that influence first impressions like physical appearance and dress mean nothing over the telephone. For face-to-face interviews, suggest the reporter come to your place of business where you'll naturally feel more comfortable.

Prejudices can pop up when you least expect it. When a reporter of Middle Eastern descent from a local paper called friend Pat Kahnle, director of Adult Education for the Cobb County (Georgia) Public Schools, about a press release announcing the program's annual International Festival, she naturally began talking freely about the upcoming event. Her program offers adults without a high school diploma the opportunity to earn a Graduate Equivalency

*"We run our newspaper 'tight' for economic reasons and seldom is there any room for unsolicited material of a business nature. If a local merchant contacts us about a new product, service, or event it sponsors, we will use that."*

Elaine Armstong,
Lifestyle Editor
***Clarinda Herald-Journal***
Clarinda, Iowa

Diploma (GED) as well as specialized job skill training and assistance when English is a student's second language, thus the inspiration for an event to recognize and celebrate multicultures.

For some reason, the reporter attempted to force the interview into a confrontation over religious freedom. "He tried every way possible to get me to say that we forced Christian beliefs on the students," recalled Pat, who obviously took a guarded position for the remainder of the interview.

Young reporters more so than seasoned ones try to make a name for themselves and, in their zeal, may hype some stories. Most do not deliberately exaggerate but in their eagerness sometimes step over into an area more correctly labeled dramatic license by adding spice where none is warranted. They too are trying to get the attention of an editor. Forthright professionals view irresponsible reporting with contempt, and chronic offenders must ultimately find other means of employment.

You'll want to avoid conflicts that may wind up in print. No reputable organization intentionally seeks bad publicity. Your business behavior should stand on its own merit and not require mere curiosity from an aroused public to get attention. At other times the potential effects of an embarrassing incident can quickly evaporate if handled with honesty and humor.

In early 1989, I had the good fortune of hearing Erk Russell, then head football coach at Georgia Southern College, address an Atlanta ballroom full of

*"The primary purpose subscribers take my paper is to learn about local people and local events. I don't have space to waste on other things, no matter how interesting."*

Edwin J. Sidey,
Editor & Publisher
***Adair County Free Press***
Greenfield, Iowa

telecommunications professionals. His address came just weeks after the conclusion of another successful season of football, and perhaps one of the most curious job-offers-that-wasn't on record.

Coach Russell served as defensive coordinator and right-hand man to Vince Dooley at the University of Georgia for 17 years before accepting the challenge of starting a college football program *from scratch* at Georgia Southern in 1982.

When Georgia's Dooley announced he was ready to retire from coaching at the end of the 1988 season, the word went out that the Bulldogs wanted the beloved Russell back in the fold. But when he turned them down to stay at Georgia Southern, University officials denied an offer was ever made (Coach Dooley emphasized to me, however, that he was not one of the officials).

In typical Russell style, the legendary coach told his audience that day of how he gladly accepted the larger benefits of a personally embarrassing situation. "That [incident] gave Georgia Southern a lot of publicity. We were in the newspapers and on television everyday for a week. So I decided that along about June when not much is happening and we need some publicity, I'm going to call a press conference and turn down the job at Notre Dame."

Controversy is not necessarily all bad. It can and does heighten public awareness and will get you noticed, but unlike the ultimate outcome for Coach Russell, it's usually not the kind of attention you want so controversy is best avoided altogether.

*Handling negative publicity*

Mistakes and misfortunes do occur and it's best to admit them immediately. The best way to deal with potentially bad publicity is to rely on what you have cultivated with the media in your quest for good publicity. Be open, be honest -- show warts and all -- and work with the media, not against them.

Public relations cannot dispel serious problems in your operation. You may hold the public at bay for a while but fallout from poor business practices eventually overtakes any gains from positive, though not altogether truthful, media exposure. It's then unfair and unlikely any media campaign can smooth things over. Demonstrate a strong sense of social responsibility by developing a tangible plan to fix the mistake and then follow through.

The makers of Tylenol were not directly responsible for the deaths of seven Chicago people who died after taking their product in 1982, but they handled the potentially disastrous backlash from the bad publicity by taking responsibility -- by giving the buying public a way to tell if their products would ever be safe enough to take home again. Instead of backing away and saying there was nothing they could do about it, they quickly implemented tamperproofing methods for over-the-counter drugs and told us of their plans and progress daily in the news media.

Their take-charge response to the despicable act of a person or persons still unknown elevated their position among peers -- tamperproofing was adopted by the entire industry -- and in the public's eye. By doing the right thing, the company was able to avoid a financial catastrophe and save Tylenol's share of the highly competitive over-the-counter pain medicine market.

Plan to avoid bad publicity just as you plan to take advantage of opportunities for positive publicity. Recognize potential problems in your operation and devise a plan to deal with bad press before it happens. It's better to have a disaster prevention plan you never put into action than to need one and not have it. Make sure to designate one person -- someone reachable -- as public relations spokesperson for your company, and inform your entire staff about the person to whom all questions from the media should be referred. If trouble does happen, don't avoid the media; you'll need their help.

Reporters are trained to control interviews. If one calls on you and you're already uncomfortable, the reporter's methods may be a little too intimidating for you to come out feeling anything but frustrated and resentful. It's ok to tell the interviewer you're a little nervous and ask if you can speak "off the record." A good reporter will honor your request, relax his or her posture, and listen instead of concentrating on taking notes.

The media's overplay of contradictory statements and suspected cover-ups can, at best, cast a shadow over an otherwise good public image. Nothing raises the antenna of suspicion, instinct, and training like "no comment." A good reporter knows that "no comment" could have several meanings: the fear factor of losing

*"I run a community weekly serving 22,000 people. My news hole is filled with local news first, then area news. General news beyond our immediate area simply does not get in. The only way to make sure your announcement or whatever gets in, unless it is local, is to advertise."*

Randy Sunderland,
Managing Editor
***Delta County Independent***
Delta, Colorado

one's livelihood; the misplaced pride of not knowing the answer but being unwilling to admit it; the ill-advised smoke screen of having a very good reason not to comment but not giving it; or just plain stonewalling by hiding information about a significant story.[5]

Although your "no comment" may not necessarily be an act of intentional resistance, a reporter has no choice but to approach it as such and dig deeper. If a reporter cannot get answers from you, he or she may call other sources, even your competition, to get at the facts.

And last, in the words of Dodger Manager Tommy Lasorda, "Never argue with people who buy ink by the gallon."[6] Altercations with the press make your chances for positive publicity ultra-slim. Being honest and cooperative will usually take a lot of the bite out of even a zealous reporter's final product, and you'll come out looking better in print than you might perhaps otherwise.

### News vs. Ads

Ethical publications strive to be respected enough to influence opinion and affect change. For this reason, news and advertising are kept separate. Don't assume buying an ad entitles you to a story, and never attempt to bribe an editor by suggesting you might be willing to advertise in exchange for running your news release. Remember, the whole object of newspaper publicity is to capitalize on the implied third party endorsement the media provides by running your news release with no strings attached.

Don't feel pressured if an ad salesperson coincidentally calls just after you have submitted a news release. Editors and advertising managers don't sit around comparing notes for long without losing credibility (one surveyed journalist admitted he didn't know what his paper charged for advertising). Besides, readers smell a rat when your editorial material appears near your ad, and the affect of your piece fizzles.

However -- and it's a *big* however -- a number of editors participating in the survey were very outspoken about the news-ad connection, so we're going to talk about it here and now, get it out into the open, and maybe the healing can begin.

Some journalists, particularly publishers whose job it is to pay the bills, really have "an attitude" toward businesses that buy radio or television advertising only to send a slick looking press kit to the newspaper and expect them to eagerly sacrifice the space. Think about it. Who wouldn't resent being hit on for a freebie by some ninny who has just paid for like services down the street?

Newspaper people watch TV and listen to the radio and they know a snake when they see (or hear) one. If that weren't insult enough, the material blatantly smacks of advertising. Lacking even the thinnest thread of news value, the editor has no choice but to dump it. He and the dimwit both wind up irritated because of a simple yet common misunderstanding which could have been easily avoided.

*"Localize, localize, localize."*

Geof Skinner, Editor
***The Gazette-Democrat***
Anna, Illinois

Surveyed journalists report they charge an average of $6.80 for this dinky thing, and that's cheap. Some charge less while others report rates of $25 per column inch and more. Run a 2-inch by 4-inch ad and that'll cost you $54.40. Turn in a good news release that runs eight-column inches when typeset and that's $54.40 you didn't have to spend.

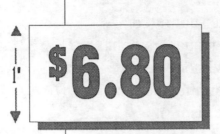

One column inch of newspaper space.

Some editors, like Richard Pratt, *Knoxville Journal-Express*, Iowa, take a less sensitive approach to the situation. "Our decision about news releases does NOT hinge on whether the submitter is a regular advertiser," says Pratt. Nevertheless, don't risk rerubbing any already raw nerves when approaching your favorite editor.

Never expect news and ads to be a one-for-one proposition -- *I'll buy an ad this week if you print a nice story about me next week*. If done properly, news stories and advertising operate independently. You'll advertise in your local newspaper because it's smart for business. You'll produce timely, informative news releases of benefit to readers because you're a good citizen, willing to share information others would like to know. Both gestures will impact your business in a positive way. It not only makes economic sense to advertise in your local paper, it validates your position as a contributing member of the community. In smaller markets, newspaper ad sales ensure residents receive both the weekend grocery specials *and* objective local reporting.

And while 'news vs. ads' shouldn't become a hostile situation, running the occasional ad in your hometown paper will help to thaw out an otherwise frosty editor when it comes time to submit your news releases. No self-respecting newspaper will refuse to publish real news from a nonadvertiser, but those who demand news coverage while refusing to advertise aren't likely to experience the real benefits of a good public image since they haven't a clue as to what it means.

Rhonda Vines, news editor for **The Haralson Gateway-Beacon** in Bremen, Georgia, explains: "The newspaper sees itself as a community servant, so it sees those who demand services . . . without ever giving back as ungrateful and selfish. They don't understand (or care) that advertising is what provides editorial space. The less advertising one has, the less editorial space one is able to provide."

Don't overlook the potential benefits if a newspaper approaches you about buying an ad in an upcoming feature section on your particular industry. In this case, an ad accompanying editorial mention of your business will not dilute the effectiveness of your news items. Quite the contrary. Round-up articles suggest you're at the forefront of your industry. Ads reinforce your leadership position. Readers may interpret your failure to advertise as an indication that all is not well.

## What Is 'News Value'?

Every news release should have a specific purpose that will benefit your business, reflect public interest, and be of value as news. What is *news value*? News value is information that an editor believes will excite the reader. A good news story quickens the pulse or elicits an emotion. It may be funny, heartwarming, or sad. It may make you angry or fearful, or attract you because of some interest you have in the subject. News value may be found in a new law, a tragic mishap, higher prices, or a medical breakthrough.

Excerpt from a guidelines story entitled *Give us the Business*

*"We like to put news of local business people into Business Plus, and we need your help to do it. If your company promotes people, if your salespeople win awards, if your industry group brings in outside speakers, . . . you can send in announcements . . . with pretty good confidence that they will actually appear."*

Steve Bills, Business Editor
**The Macon Telegraph**
Macon, Georgia

Certain behavioral patterns qualify as having value as news, and therefore grab the attention of the media if substantial numbers of people begin to display them. Every day newspapers carry progress reports of how society is being molded by the movement of trends. Intangible news reflects current thoughts, opinions, fears, and tendencies -- those things more in the air than something you can grasp and hold in your hand -- and finds its way into print many times in business and economic reports.

Editors know what makes readers laugh, cry, love, and learn, and constantly look for news that works at sparking these reactions. A great deal of a journalist's daily frustration comes from plowing through dozens of so-called 'news' releases from writers who haven't the slightest notion of what news value is all about. Editors are sick to death of purely self-serving material dressed up to look like news. Assaulted for years by "news" that isn't news accounts in part for the attitude.

Editor Pratt, *Knoxville Journal-Express*, Iowa, has managed to incorporate all the bad material he receives into his daily physical workout. "Every morning, I receive a stack of mail consisting mostly of other newspapers and news releases. Thereafter, the job is mainly 'rip, scan and toss.' That is, rip open the envelope, scan its contents and toss it in the trash."

Likewise, Robert A. Hatch, editor and publisher of *The Lakeville Journal*, Lakeville, CT, steadfastly holds onto the hope of unearthing a nugget in the trash heap. "I still open the releases and read them, hoping somehow to strike pay dirt, even though it often feels like panning for gold long after the vein has played out."

Small business owners usually miss the mark because their thinking is all wrong. By understanding that a subtle shift in thinking can make the difference between what is considered ad copy and what is truly news copy, you can begin generating the kind of information editors want.

Rick Thomason, editor of **The Dothan Progress** in Dothan, AL, offers some insight into how to make the distinction. "Small businesses and most public relations firms are the worst entities trying to pass off advertising as 'news'. An ice cream parlor that adds 10 new flavors will try to pass that off as news. It isn't news, it is advertising. On the other hand, if that same ice cream parlor sold 10 times more butterscotch crunch ice cream in one summer than any other parlor in the chain, that is news."

The ice cream parlor tries to attract an immediate rush of customers by announcing an increase in product choice. Wrong thinking. Publicity doesn't produce instant results. Remember, publicity plants seeds in the minds of the public that grow and blossom over time to yield the desired results.

Let's suppose you operate that ice cream parlor. A news release informing the public that you lead the chain in the sale of a certain flavor ice cream sends out a lot of messages to the ice-cream-eating public and qualifies as having news value . . . *the butterscotch crunch must really be good, and you*

*"If my paper isn't good enough to advertise in, it isn't good enough for your press release."*

Eladio Armesto III, Publisher
*El Nuevo Patria*
Miami, Florida

*apparently treat your customers right because they go back for more.* There's no law against working in the fact that although butterscotch crunch is your leading seller, it's but one of 25 flavors since you've recent added 10 new ones to the line up . . . *you sell more of it, prices must be fair, and now all those flavors . . . hmmm, the next time I'm in the mood for ice cream, I'll remember this place.*

Of course, one small article in the newspaper one time won't move mountains; you'll have to keep feeding the editor. And what if you can't claim you lead anybody in anything? What than? What can you say that will trigger the reader's emotions and achieve your purpose without reading like an advertisement?

Suppose your goal is to attract customers. And let's further suppose some or all of your employees attend high school and only work part time. How about a light article illustrating the valuable work experience these young people are getting? Time this type of release for late spring since getting a summer job is so much on the minds of both young people and their parents at that time of year.

You can explain several of the jobs and the skills required, and what kind of training program you use. Offering a few nuggets of advice on what employers look for when hiring kids, and what's expected after they're on the payroll, will appeal to young people looking for summer jobs.

Interview several of your young charges for direct quotes, and mention where they go to school and perhaps what they plan to do after high school

*"Most big businesses advertise on TV and send press releases to the weeklies. Neither is too effective. Most PR people forget or don't realize that many editors are also ad salesmen. Most news releases I use are from those who advertise. It might not seem fair, but it's a fact of life."*

Russell Ebert, Editor
**Van Buren County Register**
Keosauqua, Iowa

(remember, this is a career building piece). Include parents' names, and be sure to verify the spelling of both first and last. To add interest, send along a couple of action photos with your release. (As a courtesy, make sure kids and parents understand the information and photos are for a newspaper article, and avoid any embarrassment should someone object to their name and picture being published.) You should capitalize on the potential for humor here. No matter how many jobs we have in a career, we never forget our first. Incidentally, a well-done humorous treatment will always get an editor's attention.

What reaction will the reader have to the kind of piece I have just described -- *what's the news value*? The editor knows readers are curious about their neighbors -- *names make news* -- and like to read about them. The closer readers identify with the people in news stories, the more likely they are to read that publication regularly. This example shows you care about kids -- *giving something back to the community*.

Many young readers interested in summer employment may consider you a good prospect, and you'll have the cream of the crop from which to choose when they line up for job applications. Many of your potential customers will be parents, and all parents project your treatment of children -- anyone's children -- onto how they might expect you to treat their own kids. Other adult consumers will be impressed that the customer service these youthful workers provide -- *your reputation* -- is no accident.

This news release *implies* that stopping by your place for a double cone will be a pleasant and yummy experience. The editor will love your fresh, creative approach and consider the information supplied for teen job seekers a valuable commodity he or she will want to pass on to readers.

How would this type of release achieve your goal of attracting new customers? Nowhere in it do the words 'first time customer discount' appear. You haven't referenced your special Flavor of the Month or that you have the lowest prices and highest quality ice cream in town. For the very same reasons we have just mentioned, potential customers will perceive you as someone worthy of their business -- someone like themselves -- a 'real person' who stocks a quality product and cares about customers enough to teach youthful employees how they should be treated.

If this sounds simple, it is. We said the purpose of the release was to attract new customers. Actually a better way of thinking about it is "attract new customers by showing good will." A piece like this builds good will. It instills trust by illustrating you are a responsible, caring member of the community.

You're better off concentrating on other, less tangible goals than 'getting new customers' when planning a news release campaign. Restrict your thinking instead to a few basic concepts like showing good will, giving back to the community, being a good citizen, reaching out and being responsible even when you don't have to. If our darker side loves detailed accounts of blood, guts, and gore, poignant stories of compassion and selfless giving touch our hearts and restore our faith. Thinking of ways to publicize the good your business does will prompt a natural flow of ideas that can lead to dozens of news releases.

The public's perception of your image as portrayed through good will publicity translates into more and more customers. When they show up to buy, remember, it's your job to live up to that image.

## No overwritten news full of holes, please

Newspapers want your news releases but they definitely will pick and choose. Giving the editors what they want in a form they can use greatly increases your chances of getting into print. An editor is more likely to use material that already conforms to his paper's style when he receives it than if it needs rewriting to meet style requirements. Some operations have the manpower and time to rewrite your material but most do not.

Complaints by Larry Grooms, editor-in-chief of *Antelope Valley Press* in Palmdale, CA, about wordy, long-winded passages that don't say anything were echoed by a number of the journalists participating in the survey. "We run few news releases verbatim. The vast majority need rewrite, or at least heavy editing, because they arrive here overwritten and under-reported," said Grooms.

Don't leave information holes. Once, while I was news editor of *The Cherokee Tribune*, Canton, GA's weekly, a young woman came into the office and asked that we run her wedding announcement. We

*" . . . it is of utmost importance that, when a business or organization seeks publicity in the small newspaper, that [they] somehow show the editor and the reader why the information to be published is of particular interest to the 'locals'."*

Ralph B. Davis III, Editor
*The Jackson County Sun*
McKee, Kentucky

had a standard form for that type of information, as do most papers, and she was given one to fill out. She seemed oddly nervous -- not the normal bride-nervous, but more fearful -- and she appeared to struggle with some of the questions.

After a few minutes, half curious and half thinking I might be able to ease her distress, I asked if she needed any help. Without comment she handed me the questionnaire for approval. Though her answers were pitifully lacking in detail, the space for one vital piece of information was left blank -- *the groom's name*. When I pointed this out, she said, "I don't want his parents to know." Editors have little time or patience for deliberately failing to include basic information.

Sometimes it's not a case of purposefully leaving out vital details, it's simply because you're too close to the subject -- you know it too well. Though you may know what you're talking about, will someone else who is not as familiar be able to understand it? Have a friend who knows little about your business read the release. If they need clarification, so will an editor.

The editor exercises total control over placement, timing, and content. He'll rewrite or cut to suit his needs and the space available. Don't expect him to cheerfully allow you to review the changes either. Don't even ask. Such a request suggests you believe him to be incompetent. Don't ask that your release appear on a particular page or in a favored section. The editor will know where best to place it. Accept whatever space your material is given with gratitude.

*First impressions*

Perhaps the editor's first inkling that you exist occurs when he uncovers the envelope containing your news release in a hefty mound of mail. If submitted on your letterhead, the "recognition factor" will begin to payoff as your publicity campaign progresses. If your material has served his needs in the past, the editor will distinguish your envelope from the others and be curious about what you have for him this time.

Chances are he'll open it while talking to someone on the phone. At the same time his boss may be gesturing for him to hurry up, for he's already late for the daily news meeting. Will he be stopped momentarily by your headline? He had better, for if you're to get his attention at all, it must begin with the headline.

The editor is likely to change your headline to fit the space he can give your article, but a good one will prompt him to read on, and that's the first step toward getting what you have written printed for others to see. A good headline accurately and compactly summarizes the information to follow.

Study headlines in the newspapers you read for help in writing your own. Notice that each one is a complete thought and includes an active verb. (For more on headline writing, see Chapter 5.)

*Photos & illustrations*

Appealing photographs illustrating the point made in the release will also capture the editor's attention and

*"A suggestion would be for the P.R. writers to put themselves in the shoes of the reporters and editors. They should understand what we consider newsworthy and how to write a story that is factual without sounding like an advertisement. And fancy writing doesn't get you in the paper. Just the facts, . . . but don't make it too long or too boring."*

Kirk Caraway, Editor
*Teton Valley News*
Driggs, Idaho

make him want to know more. Seventeen percent of surveyed journalists report that the availability of good, usable photos or illustrations most influenced their decision to run a news release. Another 47 percent said good graphics was sometimes the deciding factor. (See Chapter 4 for more about photographs and illustration.)

### Follow-up & deadlines

Don't despair if every article you submit fails to make it into print, but if repeated submissions produce no results, call to see what you can do to make your releases more usable. The survey concludes that follow-up is fairly important to a few editors but not so much so with most of them, and overall, they report only about 12 percent of submitters ever inquire about the fate of their material.

Surveyed editors are clearly nonchalant about offering advice for improvement of unsolicited releases. Though 71 percent said they are willing to make suggestions, many do so conditionally, namely only when asked by local people or organizations. Not surprising since they report fully 18 percent of submitters resent any offer to render their pitiful prose into a usable state.

While it seems incredible, one out of 11 who follows up is neither polite nor considerate of the editor's position, and even more incredulous, a whopping 24 percent are totally oblivious to the editor's need to meet a deadline. Don't annoy the editor by asking 'Did you get my release?' He might say 'yes' just to get rid of you. Don't ask why he hasn't run it or if he intends to.

Don't ask him if he would like additional background material or a photo or illustration. If appropriate now, why were they not so prior to sealing the original envelope? Instead, ask if he has any questions about the information or suggestions to make the material more appealing. Don't be guilty of overemphasizing the importance of your release. Hard news takes priority for space.

Estimating how often your news releases will catch a particular editor's eye, fill his need for the next issue, and actually get printed defies prediction. However, following the advice in this book should propel your performance far beyond survey averages.

Contributing journalists report they consider for publication only about 26 percent of all news releases received. Some editors say they review 100 percent of those submitted while others claim they ponder practically none. Again, some qualifiers apply; having a hometown or regional connection guarantees that the editor will give it a good look, but even then some say they only use news releases as story tips, and they go off and do their own research and writing. Of course, even when this happens, it's still possible for the tipster to realize some publicity.

Of the 26 percent of news releases making the first cut, less than half survive to actually make it into print. That means that of all the news releases reaching newspaper offices all across America, only about 10 percent ever get published. Why? The biggest complaint journalists give for not using news releases is that they read like advertising, and editors are not at all motivated to rewrite them into news style since ad copy contains zero newsworthy material around which to build a story.

For their next most annoying reason, editors list unsuitable subject matter. Here again, they plead for news angles of interest to readers served by the publication. Coming in third is the limited amount of news space available. Remember, surveyed editors devote 19 percent of their news space to unsolicited releases, and of that, especially in smaller communities, much is taken up by "local agencies -- Extension Service, USDA offices, etc., and Armed Forces Hometown News," says Edwin J. Sidey, editor and publisher of *The Adair County Free Press* in Greenfield, Iowa.

In a three-way tie for fourth place with not an eyelash's worth of difference among them we have Poorly Written, Not Enough Information, and Too Technical. These three impish little characters seem to be everywhere at once, but usually an editor's provincial instincts emerge to pull them in line if they're known to be from the neighborhood. Most editors (75 percent of those surveyed) will take the time to call for more information and rewrite a locally generated release if the material is of particular interest to his or her readers.

News release writers who go overboard with lengthy, complicated material would fare better sticking to "easy reading in a short time," recommends Gail Newsome, managing editor of *The Jasper News* in

Jasper, FL.

A first cousin to the triplets, Unsuitable Writing Style, follows as the next major reason editors can't use your releases. But here again, if the information has local appeal and doesn't show up too long and messy, editors are likely to rewrite it.

Editors also lament of poor timing, useless and uninteresting information, poor graphics or photos, and lack of newspaper staffers for processing as other reasons releases wind up in the trash.

Failing to follow the standard news release format -- typed double-spaced with the words 'News Release' top center, etc. -- most often finished last among editor gripes. Almost every release writer gets that part right.

## *Chapter Key Points*

* Releases must only appeal to publication's editor.
* Gaining editor's trust leads to public trust. Develop good media relations.
* Become *the* expert.
* Think like a 'newsman' and give the editor good information at the proper time.
* Prepare for negative publicity. Appoint a media spokesperson for your company.
* Avoid THE NINE FATAL ERRORS:
    Reads Like Advertising
    Unsuitable Subject Matter
    Poor Writing
    Not Enough Information

*Chapter Key Points cont.*

Too Technical
Unsuitable Writing Style
Poor Timing
Useless Uninteresting Information
Poor Graphics or Photos

• While news of your business is the most important piece of information you know of, to an editor it's just another unsolicited news release.

# 4

# News Under Your Nose

- **Begin at home**
- **Developing a nose for news**
- **Putting your experience to work...indirectly**
- **Relating knowledge to news**
- **Venturing away from home**
- **The mechanics**
- **Photos & illustrations**
- **Mailing lists**
- **Publicity ideas**

By now it should be pretty clear that any news release campaign needs to begin with a clearly defined business image and a thorough understanding of newspaper editors and the job they perform. With this foundation in place, it's time to plan your attack. Some years ago a colleague of mine displayed a plaque that read 'Never Launch A Vast Project With A Half Vast Plan' and that philosophy certainly applies here in order to avoid kicking yourself purple over wasted effort and missed opportunities.

Small town newspapers, many publishing only once per week, far outnumber large dailies, and rigidly restrict items of news to those with a distinct local connection. Most cater to subscribers numbering just

*"...it is the local interest, or the potential local interest that can be developed from the basic release. Most often there is none, and the release is destined for the wastepaper basket. The client might as well have saved the price of paper, ink, postage and whatever little creative energy went into the writing and editing of the release. Main reason: too little creative energy went into the concept in the first place."*

Robert A. Hatch,
Editor & Publisher
*The Lakeville Journal*
Lakeville, Connecticut

a few thousand like Knoxville, Iowa's biweekly *The Knoxville Journal-Express* -- circulation 3,500. Editor Richard Pratt characterizes his publication as ". . . small by metro-America's standards, but . . . typical of rural newspapers across Iowa and across the country. Papers like ours . . . make up the vast majority of all papers published in the U.S., and I would venture to guess that our combined readership may be larger than that of the 50 largest newspapers in America."

He's right. According to *Gale Directory of Publications and Broadcast Media*, U.S. nondailies outnumber dailies more than five to one -- 9,104 to 1,735 by last count. Mega-metros, those boasting circulations in the hundreds of thousands or even more than a million, are relatively few and devote as much space or more to national and world events as to local happenings. In any case, circulation figures are seldom discussed publicly, so it's very likely John Q. Citizen has no idea, or even cares, how many households any particular paper actually reaches. It's not that newspapers care for you knowing, they're just not likely to volunteer the information unless you're a potential advertiser, then it's first and foremost.

### Begin at home

Start your campaign with your local newspaper. Hometown newspapers are exceedingly interested in local business news and make no bones about giving it preferential treatment. Most if not all of your customers probably read the local newspaper, so it's the only logical place to begin. Besides, successes with news releases at home will boost your confidence to explore other avenues. One by one and over and over, the surveyed editors hammered upon the importance of a 'local connection' when choosing items to publish, so whether you know it or not, you've already got a friend in the newspaper business.

A newspaper office is a fascinating place filled with energy. Visit yours and learn the best times to call (strictly avoid deadline periods), and the required lead time in advance of publication the editor needs your material in hand. A news release plus a paid ad, though not necessarily published in the same issue, is an excellent way to realize two-for-one coverage for a new business.  As your campaign progresses, get to know other news contacts. Make up a mailing list of them and reverify every few months to keep it up to date.

Ralph B. Davis III, editor of *The Jackson County Sun,* McKee, KY says, "Small town papers will usually jump at the chance to run a 'new business' story because they want to establish a good rapport with the business. The paper is looking for a way to attract new advertisers, so they will gladly offer space to a new business as a 'free sample' of sorts." Editor Davis suggests that information about ". . . goods or services not previously available in the area and distinguishing features about the business that make it desirable . . ." will appeal to local readers and thus the editor.

As a small business operator, potential advertiser, and newsmaker, you should at least be curious about the number of possible readers an ad or news release may

*"Local news counts for small community newspapers."*

H.B. Elkins, Editor
*Citizen Voice & Times*
Irvine, Kentucky

reach. In order to 'localize' news releases, make sure you know exactly what geographic areas the paper covers. Published circulation figures may include both paid and nonpaid distribution, and are routinely certified by audit agencies as proof of readership to advertisers.

Some newspapers claim a large number of paid circulation and a handful of nonpaid. Some register the opposite scenario with only a few paid while distributing many free. 'Shoppers' commonly print circulation figures in large splashy type right on the front page and distribute thousands free of charge. If your community supports more than one newspaper (don't count shoppers), you should send releases to them all. If you send to both a daily paper and a weekly paper, mail your release in compliance with the longer lead time needed by the weekly paper in order to meet their deadline and still preserve the timeliness of your material.

It's perfectly ok to send the same material to multiple newspapers. If one calls you about the release, use it to your advantage by calling and politely letting the others know. Most newspapers don't like to be 'scooped' by failing to cover an important story carried by a competitor. An editor may take a second look at a piece if he's aware a counterpart believes it to be of interest.

A shopper with a 30,000 weekly circulation that reaches practically everyone within miles may seem tempting, but keep in mind editorial material contained in giveaways reads like advertising (because it is), and therefore carries no more credibility with readers than the ads themselves. The publication will gladly sell you an ad and may even offer to write a feature article about your business. If a release published in a shopper serves your needs, jump on it with both feet -- just don't confuse a shopper with a 'real' newspaper as the place to wade into 'real' news releases.

## Developing a nose for news

Look at the list of business types and ideas for news releases at the end of this chapter for suggestions editors might consider newsworthy. Browse through them and note any that immediately strike you as being applicable. Some of the business categories may not be particularly suitable to your situation, but read through them all anyway because many of the suggestions could apply to a variety of businesses or may trigger some of your own ideas.

Though the list cites generalities, you should be able to incorporate your business' own unique twist into many of them.  You may be surprised to find the items listed not at all what you may have imagined or expected, but that's the key. To interest an editor, you must take a noncommercial or indirect approach -- step out of your "seller seeking publicity" mindset and step up to a different conscience level, that of being willing to share specialized knowledge. The key to nonpaid business endorsements is "indirect" thinking, and it's what editors call being creative. You possess distinct information of interest to others because of your background, study, experience, and specific business expertise. Voluntarily sharing that

*"Target the copy for a particular paper. The 'one fits all approach' does not work."*

Ward Miele, Editor
***Verona-Cedar Grove Times***
Verona, New Jersey

knowledge will produce the self-serving exposure you need and want. The list includes a few trendy subjects, but is basically just a start. It covers ideas any ordinary, run-of-the-mill business owner can develop at a leisurely pace. It's not meant to take the place of "what's happening now" pieces on the local ramifications of events, concerns, or trends related to your industry or profession. But by practicing on general material now, you'll be better prepared later should more significant events begin to unfold.

The best ideas for good, indirect news stories are right under your nose if you'll just look for them, and the starter list beginning on page 4-34 should help get you going. Once you mentally slip into the new role of advisor, your indirect thinking abilities will become easier and ideas will begin to flow almost faster than you can write them down.

The success of this kind of publicity depends upon your business house being in order. If not, expect a severe backlash. Using the word "indirect" in no way implies underhandedness. Rather, it describes a roundabout approach to selling by implying you are worthy of the business. It goes back to the basic ingredients of a successful business image -- being accountable, doing the right thing, and communicating openly and honestly.

### Putting your expertise to work . . . indirectly

You know your business better than anyone who doesn't make a living doing what you do. That makes you an expert and puts you in the position to inform

*"The biggest problem we have with news releases [as a weekly paper] is timing, . . . the release has already been used in a daily."*

Mark Hausman, Owner
*The Hamlin County Herald-Enterprise*
Hayti, South Dakota

the rest of us about it. Informational articles authored by or including quotes from experts attract readers looking for new information to add to what they already know about a subject. By interpreting trends, making predictions, and analyzing how recent events will affect the community from your business perspective, you're able to improve the reader's understanding so he or she can make more informed decisions. And you give the editor something of substance he can use to help you achieve your publicity goals.

Look at your business activities as an outsider would -- from a customer's point of view -- and ask yourself these questions: *What does he know? What more would he like to know? What will be the local impact of events occurring elsewhere within my industry? What do those outside my industry know about the effects of these events? How will others within my industry react?* Only you can answer these questions for the rest of us -- *and we'd like to know*. Center news releases around the reader. Telling an editor something he doesn't know will get his attention, and his readers will appreciate the no-strings-attached information.

## Relating knowledge to news

Items worthy of being called "news" all contain one or more news elements. Matching the information you have to share to one or more of the elements -- timeliness, proximity, conflict, prominence, economic conditions, cultural, sex and romance, and novelty -- completes the equation for news.

*Timeliness and proximity* generally warrant separate treatment, but since it's imperative that your news be both localized and correctly timed, it's best you think of them as a single element.

The timeliness of provincial news interests editors most. If it's fresh and in some way connected to local readers, it's almost a sure bet. Timeliness and the calendar match up most easily but with a marginal amount of imagination, you can come up with other connections just by observing what's going on around you.

Any ordinary large format calendar (8.5 X 11 inches or larger) denotes recognized holidays and events with mass-appeal. Though celebrated year after year, plenty of new story ideas emerge each time they roll around. Sit down with a calendar and pencil in any connection you can draw to any date. An accountant naturally links his or her business activities to April 15, a bridal consultant to the entire month of June, and a retailer to December Christmas shoppers.

Some businesses most quickly associate themselves with changes in the seasons. Landscapers and nurseries are busiest during the spring and fall while travel agents book the most trips during the summer, and a fitness center's peak period is during the winter after the holidays. After marking the obvious, start over at January and go through the calendar again looking for other dates with a tie-in.

Don't overlook anniversaries or annual events unique to your organization such as founder's day, the day you broke ground on the new addition, or a casual office challenge that turned into an annual employee contest. Use the list of publicity ideas at the end of this chapter for help. Consult *Chase's Annual Events Calendar* at the reference desk of your local library. If you can't find something in this plethora of opportunities, you're not trying. You can also simply create your own tie-in to a particular date. The following is a brief list of seasonal ideas. Perhaps it will help ignite some of your own.

*Spring* -- clean out unwanted items for recycling, sponsor collection drive/drop-off point; plant trees, donate trees for city playground, sponsor trash pickup day in conjunction with a local charity or school, at a local park or along highways; new spring wardrobes, sponsor collection of old winter clothes for the homeless or underprivileged; donate tickets to underprivileged kids to major or minor league sports events in your area; donate time/materials/food for workers building homeless shelter, battered women/children's shelter; home fix-up for the elderly; prom night; graduations.

*Summer* -- Sponsor a job fair for June grads/teens looking for summer jobs; June weddings, gifts; baseball; make available a free "be-safe summer" brochure for kids; vacation photo tips; sponsor highway coffee booth for travelers; securing your home before you leave; traveling with kids/pets; class reunions; water conservation; swimming; lakes; boating; skiing; picnics; golf; family outings; avoiding heat stroke/sunburns; accidents with lawn mowers; giant tomato contest.

*Fall* -- school begins; off to college; football; yard

*"You need to convince us you have something new or different or fascinating to say."*

James Kane, Business Editor
***The Daily Herald***
Arlington Heights, Illinois

**news elements**

clean up/fall planting; county fairs; fall festivals; arts & crafts shows; hunting season; elections; chili cook off; winterizing vehicles.

*Winter* -- diet & fitness/New Year's resolutions; first New Year's baby; basketball; hockey; hazardous winter driving; colds/flu; glove/coat/blanket drive for the homeless; skiing; building a snowman; surviving winter depression.

Any yearly happening can become the basis for potential publicity if approached from a fresh, indirect angle and given a local tie-in. Select carefully because the concept works best when you establish the event as yours -- something you become known for and the public comes to expect of you year after year.

To draw greater exposure than you might otherwise, don't overlook the potential of piggybacking your event by latching on to something bigger. Parallel your activity with an already established annual community affair, or suggest your idea to other businesses that complement yours and sponsor an activity as a group. Sell potential cosponsors by pointing out the chance for free publicity. The best success comes from unselfish sharing, and accept the reality that your allotment of the spotlight may not always be 100 percent.

Start an annual publicity notebook based on the calendar date tie-ins discussed earlier, and work far enough ahead to time your material appropriately for the publication you want to carry it. Don't assume you can fax it at the last minute. Editors are very vocal about fax abuse, as you'll discover later in this chapter. At some point you may want to try submitting to magazines which have two- and three-month lead times minimum and sometimes far more.

Keep your publicity notebook handy to record new ideas as they come to mind. Don't wait until "later" to record them. It's amazing all the things we completely forget before we get around to doing them. If you ultimately decide to hire a public relations agent or ghostwriter, you'll need to supply them with some background information and an idea of what you expect. Being able to hand over a notebook full of ready-made ideas will make the job of a hired PR helper a lot easier and should be reflected in their fee.

People are always interested in trends -- what brought them on, what affects their movement and why, and predictions about future development. Your business feels the effects of many trends, and you must constantly make adjustments to best take advantage of the good ones and to minimize any negative impact from bad ones. Trends can run their course in a few weeks or months and only affect a small portion of the population. Others continue for years and eventually touch us all. If your normally wet spring hasn't seen a drop of rain in weeks, a landscaper could develop a release based on the unusual dry spell by suggesting ways to minimize plant damage, economical watering methods, or how to convert a lush jungle-scape into a desert garden. Of course, the same articles following a flood would lack timeliness for the location.

National trends can and do have significant local interest and impact, such as the recent tendency to

*"Know your media market. Study a publication and what it uses. Don't submit what doesn't fit."*

Jane Larson,
Managing Editor
***Arizona Business Gazette***
Phoenix, Arizona

## Question from Editor's Survey

When selecting news releases for publication, do you *give preference to*:

   a. health/medical/fitness information?
almost always - 4        usually - 17        sometimes - 65        not often - 32        almost never - 15

   b. political issues/changes in the law?
almost always -10        usually - 30        sometimes - 58        not often - 18        almost never - 13

   c. minority issues?
almost always - 8        usually - 30        sometimes - 57        not often - 27        almost never - 21

   d. personal issues such as physical abuse or drug abuse?
almost always - 2        usually - 28        sometimes - 61        not often - 24        almost never - 15

   e. hobbies/travel/entertainment/leisure time activities?
almost always - 1        usually - 18        sometimes - 60        not often - 32        almost never - 21

   f. economic trends/employment forecasts?
almost always - 14        usually - 39        sometimes - 48        not often - 20        almost never - 11

   g. children or teen issues?
almost always - 6        usually - 28        sometimes - 55        not often - 23        almost never - 19

   h. the environment?
almost always - 6        usually - 28        sometimes - 67        not often - 17        almost never - 11

   i. crime/crime prevention?
almost always - 12        usually - 36        sometimes - 54        not often - 15        almost never - 16

   j. personality profiles of people in business?
almost always - 14        usually - 24        sometimes - 43        not often - 32        almost never - 15

   k. new products or new technologies?
almost always - 4        usually - 19        sometimes - 55        not often - 29        almost never - 20

**Figure 1**.

The general topics questions in figure 1 appeared verbatim on the editor's survey. The multiple choice answers and the 'votes' cast by contributing journalists appear immediately after each category. Notice the direction in which the answers lean for each topic.

keep cars longer because new ones cost too much. An auto detailer could offer an article about the stepped-up interest of locals in keeping their current cars looking better longer.

An article from a paint and body shop about new innovations and comparisons of automobile paints would interest anyone considering repainting, and a repair shop could offer low-skilled checks motorists can perform themselves to ward off breakdowns common in older cars.

News release publicity must be based on the concept of satisfying a customer problem and including the customer in the solution. Allowing potential customers the opportunity and the pride in doing something themselves builds trust. And your introduction through an informational article lets customers get to know you and your business under nonthreatening conditions.

Since news is considered factual, consumers may comfortably assess your abilities to do what they need done *in advance of needing it* and without fear of being taken. The positive publicity comes when the consumer perceives you to be the most expert (remember, newspaper coverage does that for you), and therefore the strongest candidate for their future business *because you're willing to impartially educate them on something of interest while your competitors apparently are not.* The news value that must be present to attract an editor is the particular trend and its local implications, and you'll want to say so right up front in your lead paragraph.

When doing a trend article, pick a safe and popular position that mirrors the way your customers feel, or that will attract the kinds of customers you want. Look for trends within your industry or profession, then indirectly publicize your business with informational articles.

*Conflicts*, especially major ones affecting a lot of people, usually make the front page and can include tragedy and scandal -- events that have everyone talking. While you certainly want to avoid negative front page coverage, you can very often draw publicity from these events by offering advice to victims in the aftermath, or tips to prevent the same thing from happening to others. You'll always want to find as positive an angle as possible from which to write your story. Offer a solution to a problem or an analysis of the long-term effects of the event and how to minimize negative impact.

This is where some serious planning pays off. Many conflicts are predictable because they occur time and time again. Bad things happen all the time, more so in large towns than in small, but usually it's not something that hasn't happened before. By anticipating these events and preparing material in advance, you will have time to put together a worthwhile piece that's ready to roll when events warrant.

Misfortune and tragedy generate a lot of "human interest," a very important ingredient for newsworthy material because of our fundamental it-could-happen-to-me curiosity. Many times these events -- accidents, illness, or scams -- could have been prevented, and freshly stung readers want reassuring information to help avoid a similar fate.

When many people experience lingering sadness, shock, or fear after a particularly disturbing event, editors clamor to deliver stories about the event from as many different angles and perspectives as possible, and for as long as possible until public feeling begins to fade or becomes redirected. By anticipating these events, you can be ready to respond immediately. These are some of the few unsolicited faxes editors would really like to get.

Editors may use your material basically as is, as a side story, or more likely, fold the information into a longer, more in-depth treatment or analysis. They may need to call you for more information so include when, where, and how you can be reached for the next 24 hours, longer for weekly papers (don't forget beeper and car phone numbers).

Once published, you may barely recognize your own material since the only thing to survive may be your quotes. Don't despair. You were quoted as an authority, identified as such by mention of your

*"Press releases should be creative and short. Back up materials can be furnished if editors want to embellish or change content to meet their own needs such as localizing or approaching from a different angle.*

Russ Boaeuf,
Owner & Publisher
**Dunedin Times/Palm Harbor Sounder**
Dunedin, Florida

professional or business affiliations, and that, after all, is your publicity goal.

Using the publicity idea list at the end of the chapter, let's look at some possibilities.

Every year -- *every year* -- beginning in September or October, depending upon your climate, a house fire claims the lives of small children. And I cannot remember a Christmas when a fire hasn't destroyed someone's home and holidays. It's as predictable as Santa Claus. What could have prevented it? A check for faulty wiring, space heater safety, the presence of a fire extinguisher or a smoke detector, or both? Did the family have fire insurance or a planned escape route?

You can submit your article either in advance of such foreseeable events, warning readers that now's the time to take necessary precautions, or just after when interest is naturally most intense. For an appliance dealer, a hardware store operator, or an insurance salesperson, practical advise that could prevent a tragedy like this from happening to others would be a welcomed commodity at the newspaper office.

*Ouch*. The more compassionate among us may feel a twinge of exploitation at what they've just read, and more than a little bit smitten at the thought of profiteering from the misfortunes of others. Good for you, and I would never suggest profiteering as a motive, but offering correct, complete, and well-intended advice is not an act of making out at the expense of some poor victim. Distancing your business activities won't prevent tragedies from

*"News timeliness is imperative; we seek fresh news, not histories."*

R. M. Menard, Editor
**Northwestern Kansas Register**
Salina, Kansas

happening but offering some good advice might. Accidents happen sometimes because people are careless or don't know enough to prevent them. Take the TV show "Emergency 911" for instance -- blood, guts, and gore everywhere, true, but the show boasts of nearly 200 lives saved because viewers learned lifesaving information.

Every industry has its vulnerabilities.

*"I hate to take my car to the shop. The last time the mechanic told me my new brakes were shot. Crooks, all of 'em."*

*"I don't know who I'm more afraid of, the guy who's suing me or my attorney."*

*"I've scheduled to meet with the contractor three different times and he's yet to show up. They're all the same."*

Take a common complaint or misconception about your industry and explain how you overcame it, or educate the reader on the best questions to ask when shopping around for a service provider. Consumers develop a great trust in businesses offering assistance when they don't have to. When you help a potential customer avoid conflicts over product value versus cost, what's considered a quality job, expected service life, and how to handle problems after the sale, you stand a better chance of getting the customer's future business.

Currently, anyone in the medical profession or support services can easily attract media coverage compliments of Capitol Hill. Have you thought about an informational article on how President Clinton's new proposed medical care legislation will affect your way of doing business? It's a hot topic. Everyone's talking about it (*timely trend/conflict*). An article including quotes from local medical associates (*prominence*), a couple of insurance company spokespersons (*prominence*), and even "the person on the street" (*names make news*) -- don't forget to quote yourself -- would be very well received by your hometown editor. At this writing, the proposed health care legislation appears to hold prospects for publicity for some time to come.

Human struggles such as sports contests, politics, criminal activities, and man and technology stimulate both intellectual and emotional interest. Look for story angles relating to your business based on the conflict of victory over adversity.

*Prominence* in the newspaper business refers to members of the community worth watching. Political office, certain occupations, business activities, and social status are customary root factors in deciding who gets regular attention from the press -- whether the individual of interest wants it or not. But newspapers know that names of ordinary people sell papers too, and like to include as many as possible in each issue. Include other people in your informational articles whenever you can and the more prominent the better.

Suppose for our previous house fire example, you wanted to work up a piece about space heater safety. By including a quote from, say, the local fire chief on

*"News releases need to answer three basic questions: is it easy to read, does it give the who, what, when, why and where, and do readers in the area need to know this information."*

Curt Vincent,
Managing Editor
**The Walton Tribune**
Monroe, Georgia

how many fires are caused each year in your community by faulty or misused space heaters, your material qualifies as newsworthy on a couple of counts. It's timely since a tragic blaze has just occurred, or it's becoming nippy and your release addresses seasonal fires caused when heaters are first turned on after the summer. Since the position of fire chief is critical to community safety, it also qualifies on the element of prominence.

Quoting prominent persons, especially on serious subjects, validates your material with the editor because it signals that you understand news reporting involves input from many sources as opposed to just one. Depending on the story angle, an accountant could quote a local banker or an IRS spokesperson, a driving school owner could cite the police chief or a well-respected insurance agent, and a day care center operator could repeat the words of a well-known educator or local Mother of the Year. As your news release campaign progresses and your position as an expert grows, you may very likely develop an aura of prominence yourself, and the press may begin calling on you for quotes.

*names make news*

The news element of prominence is not restricted to people. Conflicts or events surrounding locally well-known places sometimes grab more attention than does more significant information.

High winds damaged a Kentucky Fried Chicken franchise in Marietta, GA during the first week of 1993. Repair estimates were reported to be several hundred thousand dollars but the locals loudly yelled "foul" when officials of the national fast food chain expressed doubt at the merits of such an expenditure. After good natured, sign-carrying protestors filled the parking lot, the company officially put the decision to a public vote. Huge billboards challenged "It's up to you," ballots were published in the newspaper, and even an 800 number sprang into service for convenient armchair vote casting. One thing led to another, and the story ultimately made national TV news.

Ordinarily the results of such a minor Act of God would have gone virtually unnoticed by even the local press but in this case damage occurred to a well-known local landmark -- a 60-foot, sheet-metal chicken's head rising out of the restaurant roof. The 30 year old bird has for years been a point of reference when giving directions in the area --  *"Take a left at The Big Chicken"* -- and received numerous commercial plugs from other businesses which used it to help customers find their own place -- *"And hey, we're just a little north of The Big Chicken."*

Top gun pilots from nearby Dobbins Air Force Base readily admitted using it as a visual indicator when making landing approaches. Its image adorns T-shirts, an independent business opened as Big Chicken Used Cars, and a local barber shop chorus proudly became its namesake. (After the storm, traffic-copter reporters began referring to The Big Carcass.)

The Big Chicken was fun because people could have fun with it, and when age, metal fatigue, and nature

*"Information must be interesting and relevant, and information simply for the sake of promotion will be ignored."*

Mark Shearer, Editor
*The Columbus Gazette*
Columbus Junction, Iowa

catapulted it to the front pages, Kentucky Fried Chicken reveled in a windfall of free publicity. The chain fueled it by declaring, tongue-in-cheek, the bird's fate rested in the hands of the public, and enjoyed daily media exposure as events surrounding the 'Save The Big Chicken' campaign unfolded in mock suspense. Don't miss a chance to create positive public interest when places of notoriety can be connected in some way to your business. By the way, The Big Chicken will crow again. The company promised to restore the beloved rooster to its original condition.

*Economic* conditions, future forecasts, and analysis of possible impact receive regular news coverage, especially on the business page, and practically always appear in print accompanied by the word "trend" or "development." Analyze your particular industry's economic trend on a local level.

Foodmaker Inc., parent company of Jack in the Box, changed its meat suppliers, and hamburger cooking time and temperature to correct conditions which prompted an outbreak of food poisoning responsible for the deaths of two children and the illness of 500 other people in the Pacific Northwest. If your fast food restaurant experienced a drop in traffic just after the Jack in the Box incident, you could have submitted a reassuring article about your cooking procedures, and discussed the far-reaching economic impact of an incident occurring hundreds of miles away. Don't draw unwanted attention, but if a widely publicized event elsewhere is hurting or helping your bottom line in a significant way, objectively analyze its local impact for the local newspaper.

*"Press releases that are localized to our area would be more utilized than they are currently. My staff is too small to research a topic more than two or three days. So, if a news release can relieve some of the legwork, it is more useful . . ."*

Brenda Masengill, Editor
***The Hobbs Daily News-Sun***
Hobbs, New Mexico

Economic impact evolves slowly enough to allow time to watch for the effects and then report on them without losing the element of timeliness. To fortify the material's newsworthiness, remember to include quotes from other authorities besides yourself such as affected suppliers, employees, and even customers.

*Cultural* news links your business activities to the prominent customs, skills, or art of the people in your region, or contributes in some way to the improvement or development of the locals. Celebrating or becoming a part of some distinct local tradition creates a ripe environment for plenty of news release publicity. Of course, choose something with a high approval rating among members of your target market.

For example, arrange for local artists to exhibit their works in one corner of your reception area then produce a news release interview with each artist. You could even solicit your initial supply of exhibitors through a news release by proposing the idea, explaining why such exhibits benefit the community, and asking for candidates to submit applications. You can announce the premier in another release and follow up with artist interviews in still others. Even if the biggest cultural event in your community all year long is a rattlesnake roundup, find some way to become part of it and then publicize the relationship with news releases.

*Sex and romance* stories always attract attention if you can find a link that doesn't run the risk of alienating your target market. Just the other day I heard a singles club get an unpaid plug on the radio for their upcoming nude volleyball game for charity. The rules specified both players and spectators were to be in the buff. Proceeds from the $5 admission charge would go to charity. In this case, the singles club combined the spirit of giving with the news element of sex to grab nonpaid media coverage in advance of the event.

*Novelty* stories usually relate very light or humorous accounts of events with a totally unexpected outcome or consequence. The novelty tag fits episodes falling into the "truth is stranger than fiction" category where events unfold normally enough, but suddenly take a twist for an unforeseen or surprise ending.

Novelty news releases are rare indeed, but if you're clever enough to invent one or, more likely, somehow a victim of happenstance, your chances for media coverage run very high. In this instance, a call to the newspaper will usually have them eagerly beating a path to your door.

As an example, I'm reminded of the convenience store operator who grabbed a few minutes of local TV news time a couple of years ago simply by placing an ordinary collection jar at the checkout. The appeal wasn't for a sick child needing an operation or for educational funding for the young children of a slain police officer. It was for Donald Trump.

The Donald was rather down on his luck at the time and had become the subject of a series of news bits as his many lavish financial holdings began unraveling. The crafty small business owner created a successful publicity idea by paralleling an activity with a current

*"The most annoying releases come from businesses which have not researched our paper's needs or audience."*

Andreae Downs, Co-editor
*The Brookline Citizen*
Brookline, Massachusetts

item of juicy news surrounding a very wealthy and well-known person (prominence). Stuck by the humorous twist, some patrons actually deposited leftover change.

Each time you think of an idea, ask yourself *How can I match this information to a news element?* Draw a line down the center of a piece of paper and write your idea on one half. List all the elements you can reasonably tie it to and justify each one on the other half. After you finish the exercise, take a critical look at what you've come up with. Strong connections will stand out clearly while weaker ones won't have much of an impact, but every idea, like a 3D object, can have many angles so don't be too hasty to toss one out until you've looked them all over carefully.

Obviously you'll want to approach your story from its most powerful news element, but be mindful of links to any other news elements and incorporate the connection into your material. Set up a schedule of submissions noting publication deadlines and the day the material should be mailed to meet them. Soon your "future calendar" will be jammed packed and you will never find yourself stumped for an idea or frustrated over missing a chance for free publicity.

## Venturing away from home

When attempting to get newspaper coverage outside your area, it's an absolute must to "connect" the release in some way to the readers served by that publication, and it must be done in the lead paragraph. Heed the advice of Lynn Carlson,

*"The rule is if it doesn't concern us here in our rural Louisiana area we are not going to use it."*

Sandra Smith, Editor
*The Madison Journal*
Tallulah, Louisiana

managing editor for *The Brunswick Beacon,*
Shallotte, NC: "I have . . . thrown away well-written
news releases with good photos and later learned that
there was an unspecified local angle. For example, I
regularly get releases from an opera company and
theatre group in Wilmington, a small city 35 miles
north of here. Sometimes I find out weeks after I've
discarded one of their news releases that a local
person was in the cast (and the release and the photo),
but was not identified as such. Had I known, I'd have
happily ID'ed the person, put him or her in the lead
and run the release."

The Wilmington opera and theatre company is guilty
of a most common news release miscalculation -- that
it's the newspaper's job to figure out the local
connection and then state it for the reader.

And this from Editor Richard Pratt, *Knoxville
Journal-Express,* Iowa: "It means a lot to us if a
news release is oriented, in some way, to a local
angle. It might be fascinating that a new medical
device is improving the quality of life for millions, but
we would be much more likely to consider publication
if the news release about the device included
information about a local or area resident that is using
the device."

If it's not local, it won't interest the reader, and if it
doesn't interest the reader, your news release will not
get used. Editors can't read minds any better than you
can and shouldn't be counted on to finish your
material. Your goal is to make it as easy as possible
for the editor to use your news release, not make work
for her or him.

You're wasting your time and money planning a 1,000 publication campaign with a one-size-fits-all release if all but a very lucky few wind up in the trash can. Success comes from tailoring the lead paragraph to each publication on the mailing list.

With the proliferation of computers and sophisticated word processing software, it's fairly easy to set up a generic news release and then print it with many different leads. We'll discuss writing leads more thoroughly in the next chapter, but for planning purposes understand the importance of localizing the material.

Concentrate your efforts for the greatest return. It's possible that after some thought you may discover that a reasonable connection may only be made for, say, 75 of the lofty initial estimate of 1,000 candidates. Spend your time working up 75 good lead paragraphs with the greatest chance of getting published and save the paper, postage, and labor needed to prepare the others. Of course, if you can connect to all 1,000, go for it.

## The mechanics

Submit news releases on your business letterhead and limit them to two double-spaced, typed pages (surveyed editors frequently complained of material being too long). Under your logo center the words "News Release." Under that include the words "For Immediate Release" or "For Release After (and state the release date)." Then, very important, list a contact name and telephone number.

*"We strive for an all local business and real estate page each week with emphasis on features."*

Bennie Scarton, Jr.,
Assistant Editor
***The Journal Messenger***
Manassas, Virginia

Never copyright a news release. You want as many publications as possible to print it but none will if required to hurdle a copyright symbol. Give your release a good title or headline. At the top of page 2, type the words "News Release: (then the title)," repeat the contact name and number, and identify it as "page 2." At the end of the release, center the pound sign three times like this, ###. You can also use "-30-" to signal "the end" to the editor. Confine each release to only one subject or major part of one subject.

A cover letter is unnecessary unless your release announces an upcoming event for which you would like press coverage. In that case, do the inviting in the cover letter and include specific directions or a map to the event. All pertinent information should be within the release itself, including any "localizing" or so-called background material needed to explain uniqueness or significance. Rather than going through the time and expense of enclosing another sheet of paper proclaiming the special nature of your message, let it come out in your writing. A fancy looking "press kit" is not necessary either. In fact, if it appears too rubber stamped, the editor may assume 'no local connection' and therefore not give it much of a look.

## Photos & illustrations

About one half of the editors surveyed indicated that the availability of good, usable photos or illustrations sometimes most influenced their decision to run a news release. Many times only a photograph can accurately convey meaning, and pictures of local people add spice to an otherwise ordinary news release. Newspapers like 5 x 7 inch or larger black and white photographs, sharply focused with crisp contrasts (black blacks and white whites and gray in all the correct places). Magazines use a lot more color than do newspapers and may require color transparencies, so check first.

Most newspaper staff photographers use 400 speed 35 mm black and white film as an all-purpose standard. It's inexpensive and readily available for occasional publicity picture-takers as well at all camera stores and virtually all large discount and variety stores. If you don't already have a manual 35 mm single lens reflex camera, use your 35 mm point-and-shoot but, consult the operator's manual for distance limitations on close-ups. If you don't have a point-and-shoot, get one. They are inexpensive and can turn even the most photographically impaired into practically a pro. The one drawback is that point-and-shoot cameras, while great for 'scenery', are not well-designed for photographing objects closer than about four feet. For best results, position objects and people five to six feet from the camera lens.

Since newspapers usually only print one picture of an incident or event, photojournalists ignore film costs and freely snap away in order to capture the one shot that's most action packed. But once in the darkroom, technicians print each frame of every roll on a "contact" sheet so that an entire roll can be reviewed from a single 8 x 10 inch piece of photographic paper, conserving both time and supply costs.

While you probably won't be pressed into capturing a quickly unfolding event, it's still a good idea to take a

*"Ninety-nine percent of our space goes to local, regional, and state news. I am offended by the thinly veiled advertising that tries to pass for news. My trash can is filled with it every day."*

Pam Shingler,
Executive Editor
***Appalachian News Express***
Pikeville, Kentucky

number of shots just to be sure you get a good one, especially if restaging the event would prove difficult, if not impossible, as well as time-consuming. Move around the scene and take shots from a number of different angles. You're apt to be pleasantly surprised at the results.

Take a tip from the pros and cut down on costs by asking your photo processor to print only a proof sheet. Each picture will be the size of the 35 mm film frame showing sprockets and all, but the idea is to spend the least amount of time and money to see what you have to choose from. Examine the better shots with a magnifying glass to verify sharpness of focus, and ask your photo processor to crop out any unwanted dead space and give you 5 x 7 inch prints of each of the finalists. Submit one or two different shots (not two of the same subject but from a slightly different angle) with your release.

Avoid the common "grip and grin" pose -- shaking hands while grinning at the camera. In fact, make a point of having subjects not look at the camera at all. Have them look at each other or, better still, an object two feet higher than the photographer's shoulders and slightly to the right or left. If you're the photographer, raise one arm up and out and instruct subjects to smile at your wiggling fingers.

Apply the 'rule of thirds' when composing subjects and/or objects for the camera. Look through the view finder and imagine the framed area as being divided into three equal parts both vertically and horizontally. As illustrated in Figure 2, position the object deserving the most attention on one of the four points

*"A hand addressed envelope and personally signed release gets my attention."*

Don Gerken, Managing Editor
*Pennington County*
*Prevailer-News*
Hill City, South Dakato

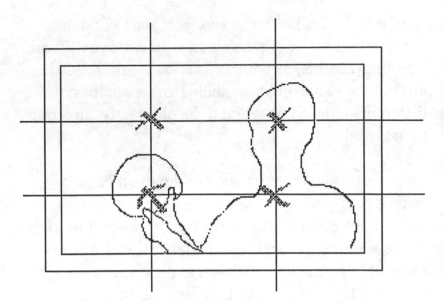

**Figure 2.**

**Practice what photographers call the 'rule of thirds' when composing subjects in the camera's viewfinder. Imagine your viewfinder is devided into thirds both vertically and horizontally. Placing the object of most importance where the lines intersect adds a professional touch.**

*"If it doesn't happen locally, it hasn't happened at all."*

Carla Cohen,
Editor & Publisher
***The Floral Park Bulletin***
Floral Park, New York

where the imaginary lines intersect. Since names make news, photos of people with objects are better than objects alone. Editors will expect all photos to be fully identified. Impeccably print directly on the back side of the photo with a felt-tipped pen so that bearing down marks don't show through on the front. If your handwriting resembles your doctor's, type the info on a piece of paper and tape or glue it to the back. The idea is to make sure the information will not easily become separated from the photo through normal handling.

Identify people from left to right and indicate to the editor that you have done so by preceding the names with '(L to R)'. Include the news release title or headline and the same contact person and telephone number listed on the release. Enclose a piece of cardboard or other stiff material the same size as your mailing envelope so pictures don't get bent, and, for the mail carrier, write the words "Photos Do Not Bend" on the outside of the envelope.

## Mailing lists

When preparing to mail releases, make sure you send them to the correct person. Misdirected material can lose timeliness sitting in the wrong person's in-basket. Refer to your contacts list, and include the most appropriate editor's name in the address. If a business editor is listed in the masthead (usually on page 2 where the cast of characters are called out), that's to whom you'll normally want to address your release. If no business editor is listed, then address the managing editor. If no managing editor is listed, then the news editor, and finally, if no one but the editor is named, then that's where it goes. Include both the person's name and title. If you can't find staff names listed anywhere, call the newspaper and, no matter how common sounding the name, ask the receptionist to spell it for you. Send only one copy of the release to any one newspaper, not a copy each to four different members of the staff. The 'flooding' technique will only annoy the most important weapon in your publicity arsenal, and do nothing to enhance your chances of being published.

For information about out-of-town publications, consult *Gale Directory of Publications and Broadcast Media* at the reference desk of your public library.

*"I hate news releases where everything is printed in capital letters."*

Mark Reinders, Business Editor
**The Sioux City Journal**
Sioux City, Iowa

This annual three-volume set lists newspapers, magazines, journals, radio and television stations, and cable systems by location for both the U.S. and Canada, and is an invaluable resource when planning a publicity campaign.

When compiling your mailing list, don't overlook publications catering to your specific business or industry found in the *Encyclopedia of Associations*, also at the library reference desk.

By all means, do mail your releases. Though faxing is now commonplace, most editors surveyed prefer not to have their fax tied up with unsolicited incoming messages. The exception would be hard news with an extreme degree of urgency -- information an editor would judge as too late if received any time other than *right now*. That does not include releases you have sat on until the last minute.

Most editor's would not mind getting a fax containing timely information relative to a late-breaking local story, but that's it. Incoming faxes mean the recipient pays in the form of operating supplies, so if your faxed news isn't red hot, it's likely that the editor will be.

Learn to make the distinction between what journalists like Denise Rolark Barnes, managing editor for *The Washington Informer* in our nation's capital, calls "fresher material" and those items not as critical. Most editors love the fax as a newsgathering tool, allowing them, as Rick Thomason, editor of *The Dothan Progress*, Dothan, AL puts it, to conveniently collect "large volumes of information

*"If not urgent, mail it!"*.

Larry Grooms, Editor-in-Chief
*Antelope Valley Press*
Palmdale, California

from out-of-town sources." William C. Baker, editor of *The Clinton Herald* in Clinton, Iowa, echoed the sentiments of many of us whose work lives have been improved through the proliferation of fax technology in recent years when he rhetorically asked, "how was news gathered in the 'old days'?"

For others, this hi-tech paper churn wastes resources and hinders more than helps -- another source of junk mail. Just as frustrating as junk mail too, since deciding "to receiving or not to receive" is nonexistent. When asked if he accepts news releases by fax, Brian Walker, editor of *The Muncie Evening Press* in Indiana lamented, "Do we have a choice?"

Bob Qualls, editor of *The Baxter Bulletin*, Mountain Home, AR, says faxes "can be a nuisance," and Russell Roberts, executive editor for northern Florida's *Lake City Reporter*, calls them "a big bother." Mark Griggs, publisher of Iowa's *Atlantic News-Telegraph*, candidly says he just doesn't like faxed news releases, while others say they flatly ignore them.

Many newspapers use a labor-saving optical character reading device to scan material into their computer system which avoids having a staff member do the keystroking. Dave Nelson, reporter and publisher-in-training for *The Hot Springs Star*, Hot Springs, SD, prefers not to receive faxes because the scanner can't recognize the jerky letters. Until you've established a good enough rapport with an editor to know for sure exactly how he feels about receiving material via fax, stick to the mail.

*"Put a name and number to call for more info."*

Brian Walker, Editor
*The Muncie Evening Press*
Muncie, Indiana

*Notes*

## Publicity ideas

Study the following business types and ideas for the kind of general information editors would consider newsworthy. Browse through them and check off any that immediately strike you as being applicable to your business. Read through them all, because what seems totally unrelated may just inspire some ideas of your own.

The list cites general suggestions but you should be able to come up with your own unique twist to many of them. Don't limit your thinking to just what is listed; it's only a beginning. As you go through the material, have pen in hand ready to jot down your ideas.

**Accountant** -- How to choose a CPA; include occupational requirements; handling personal finances; estate planning; tax planning; pros/cons of electronic tax filing; explain what to do when faced with an IRS audit, and the appeals process; small business: setting up a new business; budget & forecast; computerizing payroll; incorporations; partnerships; employee benefits.

**Possible lead for advice article about IRS audit:**
  Facing a tax audit? Don't panic. Chances are you won't wind up in court.

**Adopt-a-Charity** -- Pick a popular charity with your target market and donate a percentage of profits, quote high profile official of chosen charity; get employees involved.

**Air Conditioning** (also see **Heating**) -- Estimating cooling capacity; regular unit checks - how often are they needed and what to look for; when conditions warrant calling a pro; preventive maintenance - cleaning motor blades and filter; what to know before buying an air conditioner; understanding efficiency ratings; buying used air conditioners.

**Possible lead for estimating cooling capacity:**

Estimating what size air conditioner you need is not an exact science, but it's almost as easy as figuring square footage.

**Alterations** -- Clues to quality; save on clothing costs; fix tears and burns, methods & techniques.

**Possible lead for fixing tears:**

You've just torn your favorite shirt. Don't toss it, fuse it. This simple technique can salvage sentimental items of clothing you can happily wear for years to come.

**Antiques** (see **Furniture & Office Equipment/ Furniture**)

**Appliances** -- Considering stated warranties when comparing prices; new energy management features; getting years of service life; pros/cons of buying an extended warranty; what makes a top-notch service technician.

**Possible lead for release on comparing prices:**

Choosing between two brands of comparable refrigerators similarly priced may be as simple as

*Notes*

reading the warranty. All other things being equal, you will probably want the one covering all parts rather than only a partial list.

## Automobiles

-- *Detailing* - the importance of holding a car's value; interview regular customers, why they like clean cars; feature most 'detail-oriented' employee; be the first to offer detail maintenance contract; getting your money's worth from a auto-detailer; sponsor a dirtiest car contest.

-- *Maintenance & Repair* - getting the best price; helpful hints to making cars run better longer with regular maintenance; keeping older cars in tip top running condition.

-- *Paint & Body* - describe and compare new innovations, metallic-based clear coats, baked-on enamels, and lacquer-based paints; the endless possibilities of customizing, major versus minor work; the importance of having your car serviced by an Automobile Service Engineer-certified mechanic; preparing your car for long trips.

-- *New Cars* - matching your new car wants and needs; don't overlook financing during the excitement, tailoring a new car purchase to your budget; for budget buyers: consider gas mileage, availability of parts, reliability; for sport and speed: the importance of engine and suspension; for the safety conscious: availability of air bags; importance of undercoating; pros/cons of buying extended warranty.

**Possible lead for detailing:**

If your heart says 'yes' but your wallet says 'no', clean up that old clunker and join millions of other

Americans who are keeping cars longer and saving money.

**"Best of" Awards** -- Usually presented by city, state, or regional publications. Great publicity! Find out about available awards in your region, how winners are chosen, and how your business can become a candidate.

**Bicycle Shop** -- Compare different types of two-wheelers for intended use; safety equipment; traffic rules of the road; kids, bikes, and helmets -- quote emergency room on number of accidents that could have been avoided.

**Boats** -- Choosing the type depends on the body of water in which it's used; compare specialized accessories available such as different seating and decking materials, and how customizing adds value; pro/cons of renting before you buy; boating safety regulations for your state/lake; water skiing safety.

**Bridal Consultant** -- Compile a busy bride-to-be's check list; choosing a photographer, florist, caterer; the latest in formal wear; how to plan a great wedding that won't break the bank (mom/dad).

**Building Contractor** -- Knowing codes/regulations/ permit requirements is part of the job; the kind of contractor you hire depends on the work to be done; what to know about getting estimates and making changes.

**Business Consultant** -- When an objective opinion counts; hiring a business consultant by specialization;

*Notes*

*Notes*

measuring increased production; how to determine if fees are fair -- should you agree to pay by the hour or to a percentage of money saved after the plan is implemented?; applying a business consultant's plan to everyday work; pros/cons of hiring a business consultant to only develop a plan, or for development and implementation.

**Camera** -- Tips for better snapshots; buying the right film for the conditions; avoiding flare or calling it artsy; watch lighting; tips for pro videos; great weekend photos with disposable cameras.

**Career Day Speaker** -- Offer to speak at local high schools and colleges about your business (join a local chapter of Toastmasters to improve your speaking skills). The institutions will often handle publicity for you as part of an all-up article about the event.

**Carpeting** -- Choosing according to expected wear; light colors really are easier to keep clean; compare new features like less fuzing, trackless and semi-trackless; advancements in stain resistant carpeting and what can you reasonably expect; what's really important about carpet padding; advice on tints and dyes; compare deep steam to chemical cleaning methods.

*Idea*: Invite several kids in, outfit them in aprons to protect clothing, and turn them loose on carpet samples with crayons, ketchup, peanut butter, etc. Let dry 24 hours, then clean the samples and invite parents back to see results. Get quotes from parents to incorporate into your news release. To stage this publicity idea, team up with a day care center where

*Notes*

the kids are already present and parents will be sure to see your demo at pickup time. Be sure to take plenty of photos. (Get parent permissions prior to event.)

**Catering** -- Questions to ask when hiring a caterer; the importance of table/seating arrangements for the occasion; considerations when choosing a site for catered events; compare event sites with food preparation facilities versus sites requiring pre-prepared deliveries; discuss important considerations when choosing a menu; big event stress relief.

**Changing Technology** -- Your company just bought an expensive piece of equipment to replace an old, outdated production method. Submit a news release about changing technology in your industry.

**Child Care** -- How to choose a child care provider; the importance of telling the staff when there's a problem at home; sponsor a baby-sitter's training class; discuss your state's health and safety minimums; explain your state's staff qualification requirements; discuss use of facilities and space; explain developmental curriculum; age-appropriate play materials; piece of mind for working parents; socializing/educational benefits.

**Chimney Sweep** -- Explain importance of a clean chimney; wood burning properties, fire places and safety; why they wear those top hats.

**Chiropractor** -- Diet/nutrition play a part, too; no drugs/no surgery choices, what x-rays can show; chiropractors and your insurance company; small actions cause the most pain; tips for sitting, sleeping,

*Notes*

and lifting/carrying; specific examples of patients helped.

**Computers** --  Deciding on software first before buying a computer to run it; choices available when buying software but renting hardware; computers as more than just for games, giving children an educational leg-up with home computer; critique software packages; discuss and compare computer self-teaching methods; compare product reliability; software licensing and technical support; upgrading; advancements in laser versus ink jet printers.

**Counselors** -- Family problem diagnosis; types of treatments; implementing solutions; will my insurance company pay?; checking references and state accreditation before choosing; therapy groups, hypnosis, and biofeedback.

**Crafts** (see **Hobbies**)

**Dance Studio** -- Benefits for kids; you're never too old; recital anecdotes that illustrate a benefits.

**Decorator** (see **Interior Design**)

**Diving Instruction** -- Equipment is everything; fondest diving trips; overcoming fear of deep water; precautions when venturing into unfamiliar waters.

**Dog Trainer** -- Enjoying your pet; protection on a leash -- train your dog to save your life; saving your furniture; children and pets.

**Driving School** -- Private instruction as a supplement

to that offered to teens at school; special types of licenses, motorcycles, large trucks; driving rules and good manners; state requirements for operating a private driving instruction school; advantages for young drivers; driver's license points; passing your first driving test; possible insurance discounts; tips for older drivers.

**Dry Cleaners** -- How recycling wire coat hangers helps environment; how the practice of dry cleaning began; fur care; wedding gown and formal wear cleaning and preservation, and customary guarantees for the service; the chances of restoring fading, spots, and other deteriorations; care and cleaning of leathers/ suedes; importance of regular drapery cleaning.

**Employees** --
-- *Temporary Help Agency* - why businesses need temps; what employers want: background checks, drug screenings, physicals; what employees want: paid holidays, health insurance, tuition reimbursement, performance bonus; why some individuals choose temporary work.
-- *Permanent Employee Agency* - benefits of networking for best jobs available/qualified person; tips for job seekers; difference between employee-paid and company-paid fees, and billing methods.
-- *Your Employees* - profiles: has someone overcome a major obstacle; promotions/appointments; long-time employees; new employees; unusual hobbies, collections, or expertise; community activities; extraordinary acts of good will/good citizenship; employing teens -- training youthful workers; what they learn that they can take with them into the future; quote young workers; qualities employers look for in

*Notes*

youthful workers and what's expected of them once they are on the payroll.

**Fencing** -- Making a statement with fencing materials - choosing tips for both visually aesthetic and functional properties; compare cost of materials; building well reduces maintenance; invisible fencing for pets; do-it-yourself repair tips.

**Fitness** -- Warm up/cool down advice to avoid injury; best workouts for older Americans; personalized equipment decisions; joining a health club - costs after you join; choosing the right fitness program; relate customer success stories; pros/cons of dietary supplements; explain product labeling and include this bit of info: 1 gram of fat equals 9 calories. Without this information, the fat content of a product means nothing yet it seems to be a very well-kept secret (i.e. Fat = 4 grams. 4 x 9 = 36. If per serving calorie content = 36 calories, the product is 100% fat. If per serving calorie content for that product is 100, the product is only 36% fat).

**Fleet** (semis, panel, vans, autos) -- Safe driving milestones for the entire fleet; profile safest drivers; explain safety training, what it takes to maintain truck fleet and keep them on the road.

**Florist** -- The art of arranging; where cut flowers come from; the silk plant rage; popularity of gift basket; most unusual request; match flowers to occasion; flower folklore -- origin of names, meanings; how to send flowers.

**Formal Wear** -- (see **Bridal Consultant**)

**Frame Shop** -- Caring for fine art - quote a local art curator; decorating with framed art - quote a local decorator; special framing requirements such as needlepoint and shadow boxes; describe different framing materials/cost/benefits.

**Furniture** -- Construction qualities of a good mattress; properties of wood - protection for the winter dries; be creative with unfinished furniture; furniture making - custom versus production.
-- *Antiques* - how to recognize; proper care of; antiques as an investment; getting fair appraisals; subtleties of judging antiques; just old stuff is valuable, too; most popular item now - look in the basement or attic.

**Possible lead for mattress construction:**
    Since we spend one third of our lives sleeping, a good mattress can make a difference in the other two thirds.

**Gift Baskets** -- Advice on selecting items for: housewarming, get-well, going away, valentines, anniversaries, new baby, etc.; proper etiquette when giving/receiving gifts; why gift baskets are so popular and why anyone would enjoy receiving one.

**Coat & Glove Drive/Christmas Toy Drive** -- Make it an annual event; set collection goals; tell of campaign's success and growth in second and subsequent year events; sources for donations; get quotes from intended recipients and organization's spokesperson; for summer seasonal businesses, try a "Christmas in July'"collection drive.

*Notes*

**Hardware** -- Establish yearly campaign during National Fire Prevention Week (October) to give smoke detectors to elderly, poor - take opportunity to remind others to change batteries; 10 safety tips to prevent fires, quotes from fire chief; fire extinguishers for the kitchen, the garage, computer equipment; outline a family escape plan; discuss nails - sizes, uses; avoiding multiple trips to the hardware store to finish the job - pick common do-it-yourself tasks and discuss all materials and quantities needed to complete; types, grades, and uses of lumber; hard to find items; why people love hardware stores.

**Heating** -- Check furnace warranty before you buy; fall furnace cleanup can save you money; regular filter checks during winter mean greater furnace efficiency; compare gas and electric; buying new versus used.

**Hobbies** -- Step-by-step how to make, materials, supplies; unusual collections - quote owners; nostalgia craze - what's the attraction (trains, toys, Barbies, sports cards, Coke and other collectibles); what's involved in setting up a craft show.

**Insurance** -- Questions to ask when buying; 10 ways to reduce car insurance costs; 10 ways young drivers can save on premiums. *Bonus*: work this up into a brochure and distribute free to local high schoolers (attract kids' interest by saying parents will appreciate their concern for costs and take note of the responsible behavior); 10 ways to protect your home from theft - quote law enforcement officials, home security experts; affordable health insurance; choosing an agent - lowest quote may not be the best deal if agent skips town; can independent agents save you money; you can insure anything -- auto, home, annuities, health, fire, business, apartment, condo, computers, contractor's liabilities, worker's comp, bonds, aircraft, mobile homes, jewelry, boats, cycles, rv's, dental, vision, hospitalization; tips on filing claims for prompt processing and full payment.

**Interior Design** -- Simple, easy, do-it-yourself improvements; how to budget when hiring a professional; common problems/solutions; working with colors; advice on wearable fabrics; window coverings.

**Jewelers** -- Proper cleaning depends on the piece; see a specialist for repairs; appraisal criteria; judging quality of gem stones.

**Kennels** -- Pets need a vacation, too - a kennel is a good idea if you are expecting a lot of company, your home is being sprayed for pests, or during remodeling; in-home pet sitters versus kennel stay; the pampered pooch: extra services available during stay such as annual shots and grooming; preparing your pet for a kennel visit.

**Landscaping** -- Mother Nature and controlling yard maintenance; designs for a low-maintenance yard; chemical safety; guide to decorating your yard with trees; seasonal advice, offer to write a monthly yard chore column; types and costs of underground sprinkler systems; sod versus seed and good soil preparation; vegetable gardening tips; interview local county agent and/or college or university horticulturist on effects and recovery of severe weather on lawns, trees, scrubs, annuals, perennials. . .too hot, too cold, too wet, too dry. . . effects; bugs; diseases; how to decorate with house plants; winterizing/summerizing house plants; how to plant a tree; contact local garden clubs and offer to give them plants and design advice for landscaping a public area, a corner in the park, section of highway median, or courthouse square flower boxes.

**Laundry** (see **Dry Cleaners**)

**Law/Lawyers** -- Any change in the laws governing your business with a direct effect on the public; choosing an attorney; discussing fees.

**Limo Service** -- Most unusual request; planning that special evening for someone you love; teens and limos and prom night; types of rental agreements and contract liabilities; options available and costs.

**Locks/Locksmith** (see **Security**)

**Marina** (See **Boats**)

**Martial Arts** -- Compare styles of various martial arts and their value for self-defense; describe progression of belts and skills required; physical and other benefits.

**Medical** -- Rent-a-nurse; in-home medical care; in-home medical care supplies.

**Milestones** -- Significant numbers in production or service, for example, 'more than 4 zillion hamburgers sold.'

**Motorcycles** -- Driving laws and licenses; helmet controversy; safe driving particulars; racing; collecting; ATV's; off-road.

**Movers** -- Do-it-yourself packing tips; hiring bonded movers, additional insurance and the right questions to ask, possible coverage under home owner's policy; special item handling; storage services.

**Music** -- Renting versus buying an instrument; appraisals when selling; choosing what's suitable - how musical is your child; lessons; instrument servicing and repairs; proper storage of instruments; period and antique instruments.

**Nail Salon** -- Training/licensing needed; men like manicures, too; practical nails for working women; what hands say about you; cultivate future customers by offering birthday party special for teens/preteens.

**Nursery** (see **Child Care and Landscaping**)

**Office Equipment/Furniture** --
-- *Equipment* - questions to ask when buying; describe comparable pieces of equipment and features; do-it-yourself maintenance and when a service tech should be called; pros/cons of buying a service contract; compare buy versus lease; operating costs; fax - century old technology whose time has finally arrived, types of uses - law enforcement, shopping, dating, stock market; using a dedicated versus shared telephone line; operating costs - paper and line charges, roll versus plain paper.
-- *Furniture* - choosing new, used, or floor models; rent/lease-to-own; used trade-ins for cash,

*Notes*

consignment and upgrading; office furniture and your business image.

**Opening a New Store** -- How well community attracts new business base; incentives offered and why; quote zoning and planning officials (for this to work, pre-opening cooperation on your part is a must). Since people mentioned in the article get publicity too, they are usually more than willing to cooperate.

**Optical** -- Contact lens considerations; choosing glasses that complement your face; signs of glaucoma and simple, painless testing; common problems - seeing spots, night and color blindness.

**Party Store** -- How to plan a great one; unforgettable gift wrappings; invitation etiquette.

**Performance** -- Best month ever? Best quarter ever? Best year ever? How does your performance compare to others within the industry?

**Personal Recognition** -- Participation in community and professional organizations; contests and awards. A blurb in local newspapers and related trade or professional journals is practically a given.

**Pest Control** -- Removing what attracts them; signs of termite infestation; getting rid of squirrels/moles; what to do when critters get inside the walls of your home.

**Pet Shop** (see **Veterinarian and Dog Training and Kennel**)

**Pharmacy** -- Generics versus name brands - individual considerations; child safety; proper disposal of out-of-date prescriptions; transferring prescriptions; helps available when traveling - "I've lost my medication."

**Photography** (see **Camera**)

**Printing** -- How to buy printing, typesetting, layout, binding, and camera services; print shop lead-times; pros/cons of using recycled paper stock.

**Real Estate** -- The job of the real estate agent; common misconceptions - agent represents both buyer and seller; selling tips - curb appeal, necessary repairs; what motivates buyers; multiple listings; mortgage refinancing tips; tenants' rights in your state.

**Scholarships** -- Establish college or technical school funds for students interested in pursuing career within your industry. You set the amount and criteria for winning. Many scholarships amount to as little as $100, but any parent knows every little bit helps.

**Security** -- 10 ways to protect yourself from burglary/ personal attack - quote law enforcement professionals; how much is piece of mind worth; compare types of security devices/equipment/locks; advice on how to conduct a home/business security weakness survey; what to do when you're locked out.

**Shoes** -- Avoiding foot problems - getting a proper fit; compare types of athletic shoes.

**Signs** -- Placement and wording to help your

*Notes*

business; endless shapes, sizes, and lettering options.

**Sports** -- Buying quality, functional clothing; ask friends what they use when considering sporting equipment; shoes designed for the sport; customized uniform options; choosing recreational/professional equipment.

-- *Skiing* - planning a successful ski trip ("Skiers are spending a lot of money on their trip, and it can be miserable if they have the wrong equipment."); proper equipment - what's necessary and what's just nice to have; the best way to store ski equipment in the off-season; most common injuries and how to avoid them; survey customers for "the best ski lodge" and why.

-- *Golf* - beginner's equipment; proper etiquette; your temperament and golf; odd-ball clubs; if you're a pro, offer to write a tips column for the sports section.

-- *Athletic Team Sponsorship* -- what it takes to sponsor a team.

**Storage** --

-- *Container Store* - sponsor messiest closet contest; prize is redone closet complete with storage containers, etc.; take standard closet in most homes and solve space problem by describing what can be stored in it if organized; why most people need help organizing; find a customer, take before-and-after pictures and feature them in 'after' story on how organizing *stuff* helped solve a problem.

-- *Lock & Leave* - Insurance coverage - your agent's versus storage company's prices; choosing a lock & leave with theft protection in mind; temperature and moisture considerations; proper packing for storage.

**Telephone** -- Endless types of equipment and line features; upgrading business system with trade-in; do-it-yourself installation and safety; cellular - permanent installations versus portable; cost packages available - which one's right for you; billing - access charges plus air time; who uses mobile phones and why.

**Travel Agent** -- Deciding to use a travel agent; tips on saving money; applying for a passport; tips on planning a great vacation; little known but fabulous vacation spots; storm warnings - vacation packages too good to be true; making sure you get a refund if you have to cancel; business travel.

**Veterinarian** (see **Dog Training, Kennel**) -- Pros/cons of invisible fencing; considerations beyond cute when choosing and bringing home a new pet; keeping your pet healthy - signs of illness; shots.

**Video Store** -- Turning at-home evening at the movies into a special family night; movie reviews; understanding the motion picture rating system.

**Weight Loss** (See **Fitness**)

*Notes*

## *Chapter Key Points*

• 'Indirect' thinking is key to business endorsements.
• Relate your news to a trend plus one or more news elements:

> Timeliness
> Proximity
> Conflict
> Prominence
> Economic Conditions
> Cultural
> Sex and Romance
> Novelty

• Develop a publicity calendar.
• Use the publicity ideas list beginning on page 4-34.
• Concentrate your campaign on area newspapers.
• Give the editor good quality photos or graphics.

# 5

# Writing For Success

- **Learning to relate**
- **Think before you write**
- **Readable writing**
- **Localizing leads**
- **Using the right words**
- **Guts and grammar**
- **Tools for writing**

Editors expect news releases to report information, without puff or fanfare, that adds to their readers' knowledge and understanding of a subject. As a result, trumpeting advertising copy cloaked as news makes only a brief stop at the editor's desk on its way to the wastebasket. Good news writing employs contrasts and comparisons, transition, anecdotes, repetition, and quotes in the simplest, most readable form possible to hold the readers' interest and correctly report the facts.

Your goal as a news release writer is to communicate facts or ideas that will inform and influence an editor in about 200 words. Remember to whom you're writing, what information they already have, what

*"A well-written press release is like getting a free story."*

Kirk Caraway, Editor
***Teton Valley News***
Driggs, Idaho

# two pages, typed double-spaced

additional information they would like to have, and what response you want from them. Most editors do not require writing perfection. Fully 75 percent of those surveyed will choose a story that touches their readers, though the writing may suffer a bit, over a whiz-bang writing job with no reader interest.

Though the idea of writing excites us, actually doing it completely overwhelms most people. Though we possess the passion, at least momentarily (how many times have you exclaimed *"I could write a book!"*), we lack dedication and discipline. For this reason, many of us go out of our way to avoid writing anything. Do you ever need to write a business letter? How long is it? A couple of paragraphs, perhaps even a couple of pages? Communicating with customers, suppliers, or your banker is part of the job. You can think about news releases the same way. Think of them as a series of business letters -- drafted, finalized, and mailed -- according to a need and a logical plan. If you feel strongly about your business, then channel that passion into news releases an editor will be glad to get, and achieve the free publicity you want. You have a plan to work from so you're ready to begin.

Writing goes something like this: think of idea, collect material, find the right angle, do something else for a while, get sudden idea and write it down, think some more, plan, organize, think, write, rewrite, proofread, rewrite, edit, proofread, do something else, proofread, rewrite, proofread, proofread, finalize.  While every writer's approach to this process varies somewhat, the ultimate charge is the same: to form the sentences that develop into paragraphs that most clearly say what you want to say to produce the desired effect.

News release writing needs to be brief, to the point, mindful only of what the editor needs and what his or her readers want. After that it's all mechanics. Writing of any kind takes time. Time to think, time to jot notes, question, experience, and finally write -- a really scary thought for many people, but remember, you only need to produce a maximum of two pages (*double-spaced, at that*) and that's not so much.

If writing gives you the willies, just keep telling yourself *'No one knows my business better than I and no one can write about it better than I can.'* We do our best writing when we know and like the subject, and the more you write, the better you'll be at it.

Don't attempt to create a final release in one sitting. Schedule a break so your subconscious has a chance to take over. You'll probably be surprised at the sudden new thoughts that will pop into your head. Be ready to jot them down. After a while you'll have a jumble of notes. Read over them, group related thoughts, and then read though them again. You will notice your material now has taken on a shape defined by several main points.

Think about what you write from the reader's point of view. As you write, put yourself in the editor's place. Think like an editor, ask editor questions, become a reporter. Pretend you are face to face with the editor you want to publish your material, and tell him or her about it. Anticipate questions and answer them. New information with impact will peak the editor's interest.

*"Where people hurt themselves is when they have something worthwhile to say but they bury it in junk. We don't have time to go through the junk to find the good material."*

Robert L. Frick
Deputy Business Editor
*The Democrat & Chronicle*
Rochester, New York

Find a picture in a magazine you think looks like the editor of your newspaper. Cut it out and tape it next to where you will be doing your writing so you can look at it during periods of sitting and thinking. Just like letting a customer hold your product in his hand naturally forces his attention on it, a nearby photo of your target will work to help you stay focused.

To be creative, to come up with ideas or develop your approach to writing about them, you must let go mentally. Venture outside the lines of normal thought. Think silly or way out. The more way out or sillier, the better. The new combinations of old ideas that come out of these mental exercises may not all make sense and don't necessarily merit being acted upon, but you must allow yourself the freedom to think them anyway. Out of this flow of seemingly ludicrous and meaningless thoughts, one or two really worthwhile ideas may emerge. More times than not, you'll be delighted and perhaps even surprised at the results.

Don't wait for inspiration, pursue it actively. List your thoughts, then write about each one for five minutes without stopping. Just write whatever comes into your head. I call this exercise "think writing" and it's a good way to break ideas down into their elements.

If you don't have a computer, record each thought on a 3 x 5 card or use a plain pad of paper and leave several lines of space between each different thought. You can cut them apart and arrange them in a logical sequence later. For news releases, "think writing" is especially helpful in uncovering the headline -- the

*"I read between 50 and 100 pieces of mail daily from folks wanting space in my paper. If I can't find a local connection or something of interest for the local reader in the first or second paragraph, the piece goes into the trash can."*

Randy Sunderland,
Managing Editor
***Delta County Independent***
Delta, Colorado

simplest, shortest, most accurate statement describing the story. Try "think writing" five pages worth on an idea you have for a news release, then trim it to two pages. What's left should be pure, fat-free information. This classified ad ran in the *Lockheed Star*, the aircraft manufacturer's employee newspaper, a few years ago. The author's sentiments are unmistakable: *Wedding gown for sale, white, size 10, worn once by mistake.* Strive for simplicity to achieve mass understanding.

An element of an idea is one thought that goes with others to form the whole -- one point among several. Think of an idea as a business policy and the elements as the individual processes or events needed to put the policy into practice.

Perhaps you're faced with some nagging problem concerning your business, an issue that must be addressed before you can devote any time to preparing a news release campaign. Try "think writing" about it. You may find a solution to the problem and unearth an idea for a news release at the same time. Use this technique whenever you want to solve any problem.

While "think writing," don't be concerned about sentence structure, proper punctuation, grammar, or spelling -- just write. Uncovering the elements of an idea can lead to other interpretations or arguments you may otherwise overlook, and point the way to the best story angle. Don't make the mistake of disregarding what seems to you to be "painfully obvious." What may be obvious to you as the writer may not be to your reader. The simplest, most apparent piece of information often escapes notice and never receives a moment's thought. Giving it that moment's thought may reveal it's the one element best suited to build your story around.

Your focus is sharpest when you can compose one sentence that tells it all. Five minutes of "think writing" will produce a broad range of thoughts about one subject. Take just one of those thoughts and write about it for five minutes until you have broken it down to its absolute simplest form. You'll likely wind up with a bunch of short, choppy sentence parts, but one or two should exactly summarize what you are trying to say. With that discovery, your story should become exceedingly easier to begin writing, and you are assured of not leaving out details vital to your readers' understanding.

To achieve clarity in writing, begin by assuming the editor knows nothing about your business prior to reviewing your release. Define terms, if necessary, but use a minimum of technical jargon. Simplify terminology whenever possible or substitute a short explanation when it's impossible to come up with a simpler word. Break down the points of your argument ,or the steps in a process, so that explanations necessary for the reader's understanding of "the big picture" do not get lost.

Never use just the acronym for anything except 'USA' -- for which explanation is necessary. You know the difference between the Irish Republican Army (IRA) and an Individual Retirement Account (IRA), but your intended reader may not. Use only common-knowledge, all-purpose acronyms and, unless writing for a industry or trade journal, never anything industry- or trade-specific. As in the IRA examples, always spell out the first reference, and then follow with the acronym in parenthesis. For all later references in the same story, use only the acronym without parenthesis.

## Learning to relate

Relating thc familiar to the unfamiliar is the very basis of news or information writing. We learn by associating new information to things we already know. The public depends on journalists to ferret through the mounds and mounds of new information available every day -- including unsolicited news releases -- pull together the most important pieces, and present them in a way that relates to something already familiar.

• Contrasts & Comparisons
Good news release writers get their message across by using contrasts and comparisons to relate the significance of new information -- to add new knowledge to old. If the reader is not familiar with your business operation, he may not realize the significance of what you are trying to tell him. If the nonexpert editor understands the meaning of the differences or similarities offered in your news release, so will his readers. Tell how you are different, but be sure to explain the variations by relating them in common terms.

Developing a contrasting or comparable illustration requires you to be familiar with what's current about

*"Keep it brief and to the point."*

Bonnie Elsensohn, Editor & Production Manager
*Capital City Weekly*
Juneau, Alaska

the subject outside your own little world. Check the library and your trade association publications for what others in your field are doing, then compile information that either supports or contradicts your activities, or both, if it meets your needs.

If you've solved employee theft at your plant while others report losing millions each year, show the significance of your accomplishment by citing contrasting facts and figures. If you're planning a news release about your company's recycling program, make it part of your research to find out how or to what degree others within your industry or community support saving the environment. If you want to do a story to improve the image of insurance agents, study "public perception of service in the insurance industry."

Be sure to do your homework. Written words carry more weight than spoken ones which evaporate as soon as they are uttered. It's very embarrassing, and damaging to you relationship with your editor to make a statement in the newspaper you didn't check out and can't back up if challenged.

Collecting material is part mechanical and part mental. Once you have completed the physical work of gathering information, mull over what you've learned for how it may best be presented, then write to your readers. Apply what you learn from your research to describe a particular case. Include quotes from experts (that can be you, of course -- your first hand knowledge, experience, and opinions are valuable and unique) restating a point just illustrated. If possible, further clarify with a short, humorous (if appropriate) account of an average person's experience.

• Repetition

Repetition is another factor of learning. Using this method to repeat your message -- apply the idea, quote the experts, and tell an average person's experience -- ensures greater clarity and helps lock the idea into the mind of the reader. The reader will not remember the exact words you use unless they are hysterically funny, right on target, or badly off the mark.  Of course, you want to be remembered for the right reasons. Stay focused on the theme of your ideas because that's all the reader is going to remember.

• Transition

To further aid readers in connecting pieces of information, tie the unfamiliar idea to the familiar one by using transitional words and phrases. Transition helps readers relate by sparking our memory for the familiar and guiding our imagination to grasp the unfamiliar. Compare information by using *also*, *similarly*, *likewise*, and *in the same way*. Show contrasting information with *yet, but, however, on the other hand*, *nevertheless*, *otherwise*, or by simply saying *in contrast*.

Transition applies to other concepts such as showing that one idea adds to the one just before it. Make this connection with *and, in addition, next, besides, again*, and *also*. Help the reader understand you're about to illustrate a point by using *for instance, for example*, or *to illustrate*. Show results with *accordingly* and *as a result*. This is not a complete list of course, but I think you get the idea.

*"Thinking is one of the hardest jobs there is. That's why so few people do it."*

Editor Unknown

• Quotes
Quoting professionals or others in business validates your information and offers the reader more than one view. It also satisfies the news element of prominence, and shows the editor that you understand the importance of including multiple sources when reporting the news. It's flattering to be asked our opinion, therefore, most people will be more than willing to cooperate with a quote or other relevant material if you'll just ask.

When contacting someone for a quote or short interview, tell them exactly what you plan to do with the information and why you need a direct quote. If contacting an organization rather than an individual, tell the receptionist you need to speak to the official spokesperson. Opinions in a newspaper, other than those expressed on the editorial page, can only be found between quote marks. Anything not attributed must be factual.

Example:
When asked what she looks for in a good news release, Millann Travis Funk, president of *Atlanta Small Business Monthly*, replied, "We look for articles that are ready to go with very little required to run them. Misspelled words, though, and the whole thing gets tossed."
Editors can tell when someone has taken the time to become familiar enough with their publication to submit appropriate material. They also have other ways of knowing. "I have a very unusual first name, it's often mispronounced, but my photograph appears in every issue alongside my column. If people have ever seen our paper they would know, but I still get mail addressed to 'mister.' I just toss it out," says Funk.

Attribute quotes to yourself. After all, you're the expert. Never use the first person "I" or "we" except inside quotes. If you find direct quotes in a book,

magazine, or newspaper you'd like to include in a news release, you must get permission beforehand, preferably in writing. Most publications are copyrighted to protect against word thieves who would pass the information off as their own. However, you can get around permissions by summarizing the material in your own words or paraphrasing and giving credit to the source. Ideas can't be copyrighted. If you find something you like, significantly reword it, insert your own thoughts, and credit yourself.

## Think before you write

After completing your "think writing," gathering supporting information, and developing your angle, it's time to stop and do something else for a while. But keep paper and pencil handy, for soon your subconscious will kick to the surface and startling new thoughts will pop into your mind. This is the human brain at its creative best.

Professional writers gather facts and make outlines of what they want to say but in between they spend a lot of time just sitting and thinking. While writing involves a number of mechanical steps, what makes *good* writing is the thought put into it. Thinking gives shape to your original jumble of random thoughts and brings them into focus.

Unlike our eyes, where focus and recognition come instantly, mental focusing takes the time to think and the patience to move around in our thoughts to find the right perspective. When we're focused, the steps

*"I enjoy reading news releases, unfortunately many are too lengthy and my space is limited. I use releases that pertain to ag[ricultural] issues, health, and area concerns."*

Debbie Loger, Editor
*The Chronicle*
Odebolt, Iowa

needed to accomplish something become clear and in the correct order, and there is direction.

Effective writing has a beginning, a middle, and an end with signals along the way (contrasts, comparisons, transition, anecdotes, repetition, and quotes) logically leading the reader in the proper order of thought. Spend some time mentally going over your material. Develop a clear focus and then find the angle that will give it all shape.

### Readable writing

To please an editor, your writing must be readable. While that seems like an obvious statement, readable writing implies making a conscious effort to write the way you talk. Learning to write as you talk takes most of the mystery out of writing and frees you *to* write.

Dr. Rudolf Flesch popularized the write-like-you-talk method in his book *The Art of Plain Talk* and expanded on it in a later work entitled *The Art of Readable Writing*. Though originally developed as a guide for evaluating text books for school children, his ideas have been widely adopted by virtually all mass-audience writers including journalists since the 1950's. It's reasonable, then, that since a journalist will be judge and jury for any news release you may wish to have published, you'd do well to subscribe to Flesch's method.

You're probably a lot closer to turning out well-written news releases than you think. Newspapers

*"Rarely is a news release well written. If the writer is that good, he or she wouldn't be writing new releases, but news stories instead."*

Mike Stepanovich,
Business Editor
**The Bakersfield Californian**
Bakersfield, California

and other publications appealing to the general public are written on about an eighth grade reading level. Knowing your reader, the editor, is paramount. As Flesch points out, ". . . there's hardly anything more important for readable writing: the more you know about the kind of person you are writing for, the better you'll write."[7]

You know your business better than anyone else, and we all do our best writing on subjects we like. Enthusiasm for your business offers the purpose and the platform to make quick improvements in any writing skills you may lack.

Writing readable material becomes easier when it's aimed at a specific segment of the population -- for instance, newspaper editors. Aircraft manufacturers know their hardware is maintained by mechanics who all have about the same level of education plus a high degree of specialized training. Therefore, aircraft maintenance manuals are written to that elite group of individuals in a style and at a reading level they can best understand. Safety demands it.

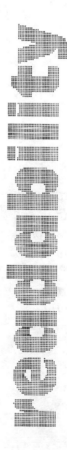

Likewise, mail order companies do a superior job of making their order forms reader-friendly. As the literal lifeline to survival, mail order houses realize potential buyers refuse to suffer an order form that requires any study. When it's critical to survival, business or otherwise, writers make a conscious effort to communicate clearly.

On the other hand, it's unfortunate that writers of insurance policies, income tax forms, legal contracts for consumers, and, of course, VCR operator's manuals never consider readability. Here the burden falls on the reader to fill in the blanks by other means. Rarely satisfied, he's left feeling frustrated and vulnerable.

Eloquence is out; plain is in. Those who deliver their message with few words are described as being plain spoken. They don't waste words; therefore, when they do speak others listen. His straightforward style of speaking explains, in large part, Ross Perot's appeal. A young man's comments during Perot's summer as a declared/undeclared/redeclared presidential candidate explains why: "When he talks, he speaks to me." Likewise, your writing should speak to the reader.

While actually writing like we talk is neither really attainable nor desirable, the theory is more of a practical way of thinking about information writing that helps us focus on delivering the most confusion-free material possible. Conversational speech is loaded with partial sentences, slang, "ah's" and "you-know's," and repetition. If you actually wrote exactly as you talked it would be too difficult for a reader to follow. Expressions, gestures, and tone of voice between speaker and listener during normal conversation help make up for incomplete sentences brought on by an average person's jerky, sometimes disorganized thought process.

A friend once came to me for help in writing a short piece requested by her daughter's college sorority for an upcoming ceremony to honor graduating seniors. The piece was to be a message of support and a wish for success.

*"Our greatest strength and our first priority is news and information for and about the local communities we serve. News releases whose writers make the effort to put information into the local context stand a better than even chance of being published."*

Larry Grooms, Editor-in-Chief
*Antelope Valley Press*
Palmdale, California

"What do you want to say?" I asked, and with pad in hand, I jotted down her thoughts.

"I want to tell her...ah...that her life is like...ah...you know, like a blank check and that, that only she can cash. I want to tell her that my gift...that, as her mother, my gift is my signature [*pause*] my endorsement, as a symbol of support for whatever she chooses. She has...ah...I want her to have all the latitude she needs to write it to whatever her heart desires and...ah...in whatever amount. I'm behind her a hundred percent." Then she said, "That's what I want to say but I don't know how."

"You just said it," I replied, "here, let me show you." To her daughter's delight, this was the "message from mom" she received the morning of her graduation.

*Michelle, your life is like a blank check that only you can cash. As your mother, my gift to you as you graduate from college is my signature as a symbol of my full endorsement and support. You have all the latitude in the world to write your life's check to whatever fulfills your heart's desire, and in any amount you choose. I'm behind you one hundred percent. Love, mom.*

Simple, direct, easy to read. Most people don't realize they already have the ability to write well.

Readable writing retains all the naturalness of speech but leaves out the excess blather; it appeals to the reader's interest by engaging his "inner voice" in close conversation rather than reducing his involvement to that of a distant listener as does a more formal writing style. To achieve readability, conversational writing employs contractions and more simple words than

| Contraction | Short For |
|---|---|
| I'm | I am |
| I've | I have |
| I'll | I will |
| I'd | I would |
| you're | you are |
| you've | you have |
| you'll | you will |
| you'd | you would |
| he's | he is |
| he'll | he will |
| he'd | he would |
| she's | she is |
| she'll | she will |
| she'd | she would |
| it's | it is |

Note: While *it's* is a contraction, *its* isn't, and many people are unsure of when to use which one.
it's — use anytime you mean 'it is': *It's a far cry from the way things used to be.*
its — show possession: *XYZ Company credits its employee training program for the change.*

| | |
|---|---|
| we're | we are |
| we've | we have |
| we'll | we will |
| we'd | we would |
| they're | they are |
| they've | they have |
| they'll | they will |
| they'd | they would |
| aren't | are not |
| isn't | is not |
| wasn't | was not |
| weren't | were not |
| haven't | have not |
| hasn't | has not |
| hadn't | had not |
| won't | will not |
| wouldn't | would not |
| shouldn't | should not |
| can't | cannot |
| couldn't | could not |
| don't | do not |
| doesn't | does not |
| didn't | did not |
| here's | here is |
| where's | where is |
| how's | how is |
| what's | what is |
| who's | who is |
| let's | let us |

complex ones, and it's the easiest and most interesting to read. Your normal everyday speech is full of contractions. How often do you say "do not" instead of "don't" or "will not" instead of "won't?" Using the more common forms in your writing will contribute to the colloquial style you're looking for.

You don't want to use contractions every time. Reading aloud what you have written will help you to decide where to use them and where to substitute the more formal version. If it sounds ok to your ears then go with it. Hint: The noncontracted version is most often used for emphasis.
Example:

*You can't go.*          -- contracted version

*You cannot go.*         -- noncontracted, much stronger

Knowing when to use which version becomes obvious (parents of teenagers can relate to this example) when you clearly understand the message you want to deliver.

To help understand readable writing or write-like-you-talk, let's look at how not to do it. Ordinary business correspondence, some of the worst writing in the world, bores past the pain threshold with wordy passages and stiff language. Unfortunately most of us were taught only the more formal style of writing in school. We learned that to please our teachers we had to use complex words and avoid any writing remotely similar to natural speech. A lot of useful information gets overlooked because it's written in a more formal writing style than readers can bear. Perhaps the writer gets so caught up in sounding "highfalutin" that he misses the needs of the intended reader. Anyway, back to sorry business letters. . .

**Pursuant to our telephone conversation of February 12, please forward all billing records relevant to XYZ Company's account for the period in question. Ascertaining these documents will satisfy requirements in an effort to clear up this matter. Needless to say, the sooner these documents are received, the more rapidly this issue can be resolved. (54 words)**

*Please* . . . give me a break.

**Per our February 12 telephone conversation, please forward all XYZ Company billing records for the period in question. As soon as the documents arrive, we're confident we can quickly resolve this issue. Thanks for a speedy reply. (38 words)**

Some would fight to the death defending the proper and correct honor of the first passage; however, it's not a question of being proper or correct that causes me to wince. It's the real life fact that people are quite simply too busy for much of anything formal these days. With the tons of written messages competing for our time everyday, we're simply more willing to read and respond to short pleasant chatter than drafty, alienating lectures.

The second version makes the same request using 14 fewer words and has a much more pleasant tone. Life moves too fast for most of us to indulge in long-winded passages, especially when we're expected to do something in return. Newspaper space is so precious it's simply not tolerated.

Wordiness results from being too lazy to write tight. Trite phrases such as "needless to say" or "it goes without saying" or "it boils down to" or "the kicker is" creep in because we've heard them over and over and said them over and over, and thus they become the first thing we think of. The ones most harped on by business writing improvement experts are the ones we see most often. If something is so obvious as being "needless to say," then don't waste words pointing it out. If "it goes without saying," then why bring it up? You may get by with using overworked phrases in a business letter, but you're wasting your time sending out news releases this way.

Lazy writing lacks originality. The writer wastes words to save time, imitating others rather than creating his own. He does not bother to take the time to think of a more original way of expressing the same idea. Interesting material moves along fast enough to keep it interesting. When "think writing," get your thoughts on paper any way you can, but rewrite them so that action verbs take the place of passive ones. You can't avoid passive voice altogether, but keep it to a minium, opting instead for vigorous active verbs to help shorten sentences, increase the pace and clarity of your story, and keep it interesting.

Passive verbs act on the subject but sometimes it's hard to tell who's doing the acting.

**Data on a client is entered into the computer and then can be printed out for his own records. (19 words)**

From this sentence it's not clear who enters the data or initiates the printout. Passive voice in this sentence -- "is" and "can be."

**A clerk enters client data into the computer then prints a copy the customer can keep for his own records. (20 words)**

*"If there is no local handle on how it applies to the community . . . it won't be used."*

Stephen Millard, Editor
***Park County Republican & Fairplay Flume***
Bailey, Colorado

This rewrite removes any confusion. Active voice -- "enters" and "prints" -- improves this example.

Action verbs can help reduce the amount of words needed to make your point.

**Roland believes the company's new employee training program is responsible for the recent upturn in profits. (16 words)**

**Roland credits the company's new employee training program for the recent upturn in profits. (14 words)**

In the shorter, second sentence, using the word "credits" eliminates "believe" and "is responsible" making for more interesting reading without losing the message. Readability will influence the editor's decision about your news release, and it's critical that you deliver an interesting message that is easy to understand.

## Localizing leads

All newspapers are partial to any story with a local flavor. Readers who never left home like to know about the activities of native sons living elsewhere. They like keeping up with old friends, school chums, and former residents, and you should take full advantage of each and every opportunity to localize in the lead paragraph since it virtually guarantees the item will be published.

If you neglect to mention that you're a native of Rockland, MA until the eighth paragraph of your release addressed to *The South Shore News*, you run the risk of the local connection being overlooked by busy Editor Rachael Jarvinen, and the news release being trashed. Since it's the most important, the lead paragraph should be left until last to write. Toy with it, jot notes about it, and rough out the particular news elements present, but don't try to finish a lead paragraph before proceeding with the rest of the release. As you will no doubt learn, the last thing a writer discovers is what should go first.

A strictly local business with local customers makes localizing releases easy, but it becomes more of a challenge when a publicity campaign involves "long-distance" publications. Start with yourself. Did you grow up there? Go to school there? Work in the area for a while? Marry a native? Did your parents ever live there? You may be able to cite but one location which satisfies the answer to each of these questions, or you may be able to list five. If you can conceivably draw customers from all five, work the localizing information into the lead paragraphs of your news release for each publication serving those areas.

Addressee: The Huntsville Times, Huntsville, AL

**Debbie Rogers Rankin, a 1967 graduate of Huntsville High School, was a featured artist at the Science Fiction and Visionary Art Show in Atlanta this week. Ms. Rankin showed her art at the two-day festival which attracted New Age and Star Trek fans from throughout the Southeast. Her work was chosen for display from among several hundred applicants. Ms. Rankin now lives in the Atlanta area.**

Addressee: The Fauquier Times-Democrat, Warrenton, VA

**The daughter of a Warrenton couple was among fifteen selected artists to show her work at the Science Fiction and Visionary Art Show in Atlanta this week. Debbie Rogers Rankin, daughter of Jack and Deenie Rogers, showed her art at the two-day festival which attracted New Age and Star Trek fans from throughout the Southeast. Ms. Rankin's work was chosen from among several hundred applicants. She now makes her home in the Atlanta area.**

Addressee: The Miami Herald, Miami, FL.

**Former Miami resident, Debbie Rogers Rankin, who once made her home in the Kindell area of northeast Miami, was among fifteen selected artists to show her work at the Science Fiction and Visionary Art Show in Atlanta this week. Ms. Rankin's work was chosen from among several hundred applicants. She now lives in the Atlanta area.**

Addressee: The Middleboro Daily News, Middleboro, KY

**Jay LeCompte of Louisville, owner of Golden Voyage, a New Age bookstore in Middleboro, took part in the Science Fiction and Visionary Art Show in Atlanta this week. Ms. LeCompte joined her sister, Atlanta New Age artist Debbie Rogers Rankin, for the two-day festival which attracted New Age and Star Trek fans from throughout the Southeast. Ms. Rankin's work was chosen for exhibit from among several hundred applicants.**

Debbie wants to draw interest for the sale of her paintings from New Age enthusiasts around the country. Except for the lead paragraphs and some additional material about her sister for the Middleboro release, the remainder of her news releases to all four publications read exactly the same.

Capture the editor with your lead paragraph, for if you don't do it here you won't have another chance. Busy editors may read only the lead before deciding it's not worth going farther, and into the trash it goes. Journalists know news releases with a poor beginning aren't apt to get any better. Your lead must guarantee certain satisfaction for continuing and then deliver on that promise. Never send out a release until you're sure it begins with the best lead you can possibly give it. What you're shooting for is a sentence or two with a promise so irresistible, that an editor will want to read on.

Rewrite your lead two dozen times if that's what it takes to localize it and summarize the rest of the story. When you've got what you think is a killer opening,

*"As a news editor for a weekly newspaper, my time is very limited. I usually average 15 to 30 seconds per unsolicited news release in determining any interest."*

Lonny Thiele, News Editor
*Linn County News*
Pleasanton, Kansas

let it rest a day or so and then reread it. You might be surprised at how different it sounds than when first committed to paper. If it still makes you tingle, go with it. If not, continue the rewrite cycle.

Make sure leads include what the trade calls the five W's -- who, what, when, where, and why, and sometimes how -- information vital to every news story's lead paragraph. The story itself will dictate which of the six questions are most important and therefore, what piece of information should appear first. While there is no set formula for lead paragraph writing, its length -- either a single sentence or several -- can only be determined by the story's complexity.

**Nurses Now, Inc., a new home medical care company, is happy to announce it is now providing both a nurse and the necessary equipment for the proper care of patients. The service will help families who must find a home nursing service and then look elsewhere for a rental service providing the extra things a homebound patient often needs.**

This 'passive' lead lacks punch and does little to pull the reader in and make him want to read on. Besides, it sounds like advertising copy.

**A new home medical care company based in Roswell has taken the trend toward home nursing one step further by not only supplying the nurse, but everything from wheelchairs to hospitals beds. Nurses Now Inc. President Henry Robinson says this one-stop-shopping concept frees families from the ordeal of first finding a home nursing service, and then searching elsewhere for the extra things a homebound patient often needs.**

In this grabber lead, the writer makes sure the reader understands the significance of in-home medical care by employing the word "trend," and localizes by mentioning the name of the town. The company's owner proclaims his uniqueness by announcing he's

*"Give it a local tie-in and keep it short and simple."*

Bob Qualls, Editor
***The Baxter Bulletin***
Mountain Home, Arkansas

not only at the forefront of a major trend but a pioneer in how the industry is likely to evolve.

In going beyond rent-a-nurse, his customers get the nurse plus related equipment and supplies. (Remember, rather than using the word "unique," let it come through in your writing.) And finally, the writer humanizes this piece with the phrase "frees families from the ordeal," something to which readers caring for the sick at home will immediately relate.

His promise of one-stop-shopping convenience not found elsewhere alerts the editor that this is a brand new service never before available in the community. It also signals potential customers that the company understands their needs, an important first step toward building the trust necessary for customer response. The writer manages to accomplished all of this including the five W's (well, 4 W's -- the 'when' for this particular story is immaterial) in just two sentences.

Unlike any other type of writing, news writing starts off with a broad brush delivery of the whole message in the first couple of sentences, then gradually narrows in focus for more detailed treatment of the information in the succeeding paragraphs. This "inverted pyramid" type of writing developed during the Civil War, but is still used today as the best way to get as much information in as small a space as possible.

If you've ever wondered how newspapers are able to make all those complete sounding articles fit around the photographs and advertisements with no space left over, all the credit goes to the inverted pyramid. The articles sound complete because inverted pyramid writing presents information in descending order of importance. Any article may be hurriedly cut beginning with the last paragraph until it's short enough to fit the space allotted for it and yet remain complete. Cuts may be made at the end of a paragraph, at the end of a sentence, or even within a sentence as long as the surviving portion contains a complete thought; thus only the least significant details wind up on the newspaper's paste-up room floor.

At least 70 percent of any newspaper is filled with advertising; ads are made up, go in first, and are never cut since the ad buyer pays for a specified amount of space. The 30 percent more or less left over is called the news hole. Though *The New York Times*' age-old slogan, "All The News That's Fit To Print," implies a high degree of moral responsibility, physical space forces journalists to print only all the news that fits (publications choose what to print based on their own philosophy of what's moral). Your goal is to write so well that the editor cuts another story so he can print all of yours.

## Using the right words

Don't try to write something you don't understand. Sounds strange, I know, but very often when I don't understand something I've read, it's because the writer didn't either and, therefore, couldn't explain it to me. Use language appropriate to the subject that readers can understand. Be accurate. Faulty language

*"I can't remember the last time I was able to run a news release without having to rewrite it to put the local angle in the lead."*

Lynn Carlson, Managing Editor
*The Brunswick Beacon*
Shallotte, North Carolina

and spelling will cause the editor to surmise, with good reason, that you may have treated the facts with the same lack of care.

Do you recognize this familiar nursery rhyme?

Three unsightly rodents, three unsightly rodents,
See how they preamble, see how they preamble,
They all chased after the agriculturer's spouse,
She cut off their prehensiles with a kitchen utensil,
Did you ever witness such a spectacle in all your existence as
three unsightly rodents, three unsightly rodents.

Instead of relying on the plain English well within his grasp to communicate the message, the writer tries to wow the reader with his smarts. He winds up looking foolish and condescending and we don't understand what it is he's trying to say. The motive behind this version of Three Blind Mice is, like the author, unknown to me but I suspect he or she playfully puffed the piece to exaggerate how not to write.

The writer uses the word "unsightly" to mean without sight. He intends to describe the rodents as being blind, but mistakenly calls them ugly instead. He uses "preamble" to describe the rodent's movement. Preamble means to precede, to go before, not *proceed* as to go forward. And we all know that rodents don't proceed anyway, they run; it's simple, direct, and best expresses the swift action of pursuit.

We could go on but this fractured version demonstrates a common error -- using complex words when simple ones will do. Flesch recommends splitting or replacing words with prefixes like *pre*, *de*, *un* and *re* and suffixes like *ization*, *ality*, and *ousness*.

Watching for these culprits will greatly improve your new releases. Of course, for our Three Blind Mice example, the writer not only loaded the piece with complex words, but also misused them.

As Mark Twain once noted, "The difference between the right word and almost right word is the difference between lightning and the lightning bug." Part of being smart means knowing what you're dumb at. God created the dictionary and thesaurus because no one can remember all that stuff. If you don't own a good copy of each, put them on your shopping list. Pro writers wouldn't think of being without them and you shouldn't either.

For news releases and other business writing, use complex words sparingly and the alternatives listed here more often.

| Commonly Used | But This May Be Better |
|---|---|
| preliminary | early |
| provide | give |
| require | need |
| participate | join in |
| possess | own |
| development | result |
| orient | locate |
| occurrence | event |
| observe | see |
| neutralize | offset |
| utilize | use |
| modification | change |
| optimal | best |
| commence | begin |
| facilitate | help |

Don't use the word 'there' at all.

## Guts and grammar

You're probably in need of a little grammar therapy about now. Repeat after me -- *I am not afraid of grammar*. Again -- *I am not afraid of grammar*. Feel better? Good. Throwing off the shackles of fear about grammar will also free you to begin writing. Don't get me wrong, correctness of grammar in news releases is very important, but good writing has very little to do with what's formally correct. Besides, grammar is mechanical, and help with that is available at the library or through friends, from trained journalists or professional editors.

Writing is thought. Do not allow your inability to recite grammar rules word for word put you in a deep freeze. Those who avoid writing for fear of breaking rules sell themselves short and deprive potential readers. Ordinary nonfiction readers are more interested in the subject matter and what you might know about it that they don't. Likewise, editors don't go around quoting grammar rules. Oh, a few forsake content for commas, but accept the hazard and go on. The important thing is to write so that it's readable.

Reading news releases in your local newspaper serves as a good springboard to writing your own. Pick out some articles you like and then ask yourself what makes them interesting. Read them again, but this time look at how they were written rather than what was said. If you're having difficulty getting started, read something similar to what you would like to write. Read your paper's business section, or anything nonfiction, and note those items that strike you as good writing. With a little study, you'll soon be able to

*"Businesses spend too much money hiring public relations firms to do news releases for them when anyone in the company, someone with a typewriter like a secretary, could do it. Before you do any major work, call us, tell us what you have in mind and we'll let you know if we're interested. A lot of people are intimidated to call, but we get things we don't want because people don't call."*

Robert L. Fricks
Deputy Business Editor
**The Democrat & Chronicle**
Rochester, New York

recognize well-done passages and understand what makes them noteworthy.

Since you will submit your first release to your local newspaper, begin looking at its *style* of writing. Can you discern a consistent pattern in the way material is reported? In the way it's presented? Is there a certain manner of word usage that appears over and over? If so, incorporate this style into your releases. The less editing your material requires from the editor, the greater your chances of being published. By copying the paper's style, you also cue the editor you've taken the time to become familiar with his publication.

Most newspapers use the *Associated Press Style Manual* as a guide for consistency on certain hard and fast rules, but also stray from it where flexibility allows for personal preference. The "AP style manual," as it's commonly called, serves as a dictionary of sorts for the proper and consistent usage of names, titles, and commonly repeated types of written material. For instance, newspapers like to be very consistent about things like time. The AP spells out that time should be written 4 p.m., not 4 P.M., 4 pm, or 4 o'clock p.m.

Occupational titles begin with a capital when they appear before the name, but are written in all lower case when coming after the name, as in the following examples:

**Hodgenville franchise President Roy Taylor's expansion plan calls for hiring 60 new workers beginning in May.**

**When asked about job opportunities for the planned expansion, Roy Taylor, president of the Hodgenville franchise, said the new addition would put 60 people to work with hiring scheduled to begin in May.**

*My pet peeve on news releases is the follow-up call from a sender who doesn't read my newspaper, but wants to know if I'm going to use the release."*

Larry Grooms, Editor-in-Chief
*Antelope Valley Press*
Palmdale, California

Though hefty as a college textbook, most of what's in the *Associated Press Style Manual* won't apply to your news release, but spend a half hour in the library browsing though a copy to get a feel for what it does. Consistency in the newspaper business saves words, fewer words save space, and space is money.

## Tools for Writing

Like every job, writing becomes easier with the right tools. Paper and pencils will do the job adequately enough, but with a computer and a good, all-around word processing package, you'll become a better writer faster. The "cut and paste" feature of word processing software allows dozens of seemingly isolated and independent thoughts to be easily arranged and rearranged, pared down or beefed up any number of times until an order and sense begin to take shape. More and better writing software packages are becoming available. Some even come packaged as part of word processing programs complete with a built-in dictionary and thesaurus.

Several good writing programs on the market will check sentence structure, flag excessive use of passive voice, plus check spelling. It's like having a good editor at your side. However, you can't substitute all that electronic help for the final ok by the human ear. When you think you're finished, read your release aloud to see if your writing is understandable and has really achieved the sound of natural speech.

Break down the job of writing your news releases into manageable bits and do the easy parts first. Don't try

*"News releases must be double space for editing – which is almost always needed, usually to conform to our style."*

Jed Dillingham, Editor
***The Dawson Springs Progress***
Dawson Springs, Kentucky

to or expect to write, spell, or punctuate perfectly in the beginning. Just get your ideas on paper; you can refine and rearrange them later. Take lots of breaks. You'll be surprised at how that difficult passage will somehow work itself out given a brief rest. Be prepared for a finished piece of writing to take more time than you think it will or should. If you manage to grind out only two sentences in a hour, don't fret; rather feel gratified that those two are behind you and you can start on the next two. It's the nature of the beast.

As someone once said (and I wish I could remember who) "Writing is slow, tedious, agonizingly difficult work for 90 percent of all writers. The other 10 percent are no doubt lying."

## Chapter Key Points

• "Think write" to break idea down into its most basic elements and to reveal the best headline.
• Relate information to the familiar be using contrasts and comparisons, transition, repetition, anecdotes, and quotes.
• Use common words and phrases to achieve readable writing.
• Don't allow fear of violating grammar rules keep you from writing.
• Localize the lead paragraph.
• Keep news releases brief and to the point.

# 6

# Managing Success

Where any notion that newspaper publicity was once out of reach, I hope at this stage you have a tangible list of ideas ready to put into play, or at least the beginnings of some preliminary "think writing" notes, and a vigorous outlook. Begin looking forward to joining the ranks of the published few.

Once your first release appears in print, besides admiring it for a week or so and tacking it up on the bulletin board, begin to take advantage of its inherent quality to produce more publicity.

Prepare a presentation notebook and show it to prospective customers --"the media is talking about us" -- and include it with other sales literature for

*". . . tell the reader 'what's in for me'."*

Sarah Bondurant, Editor
***The Democrat***
Senatobia, Mississippi

direct mailings. Always preserve the identity of the endorsing publication. Never dilute its effect by reproducing the story partially covered with an advertising message or anything else.

Emphasize the importance of editorial mention by enlarging the release to many times its original size and displaying it as a trade show prop. Look for imaginative ways to build on and perpetuate the exposure with each succeeding published release.

Measuring the success of an ongoing publicity campaign means it's necessary to establish a starting point of current conditions against which to compare future performance. But arriving at an accurate calculation will be difficult, at best, considering such intangibles as good will and credibility. However, after a sustained period of submissions, you should begin to see increased sales and then it will be easier to compare this new data to previous figures.

A prolonged commitment to your news release campaign promises increased credibility for your business image, heightened name recognition, gradual elevation to expert status and, best of all, more and better customers. It's not too soon to start planning how you'll handle them. Will you depend on family members stepping in to give you a hand, contract with a temporary personnel agency, hire full time employees, automate manual processes, or develop some combination of these to meet your needs? All are viable solutions, depending on your situation, and your business plan should be updated to include a contingency proposal in anticipation of future growth.

Once again, publicity begets publicity. The more you send out, the more that will come back to you. Higher visibility will prompt requests from all sorts of individuals and organizations depending on the position taken in your releases. Anticipate being asked for a lot of favors and be prepared to say "no" when you have to, but be careful. Saying "no" to the wrong group could cause a backlash of negative publicity. Also be prepared for some jealousy. Publicity makes you a public figure prone to envy and gossip, and you can't be too thin-skinned.

## Afterword

This book is not meant to be the last word on news release publicity. More can be learned and, over time, trends and market conditions will change and techniques will have to change along with them to keep up. But with your help, we can make this the single most comprehensive reference guide on the subject.

I am interested in how this material helps you and how you think it can be improved. Send published releases and a note about how they worked to me at Franklin-Sarrett Publishers, 3761 Vineyard Trace, Marietta, GA 30062 USA.

If I use your material, you'll be notified so you can look for yourself in future revisions. That's another way a printed release can multiply publicity for your business. Good luck!

*"Follow up is very important – polite and non-intrusive."*

Millann Travis Funk,
President & Editor
***Atlanta Small Business Monthly***
Atlanta, Georgia

## Chapter Key Points

• Use published releases in creative ways for greater exposure.

• Establish a starting point for measuring the success of your news release campaign.

• Plan how you will handle the increase in business and notoriety.

• Send published releases to:

      Franklin-Sarrett Publishers
      ATTN: Kay Borden
      3761 Vineyard Trace #100
      Marietta, GA 30062 USA

# Appendix

Truly authorship by committee, this book would not have been possible without the contributions of these professional journalists. This homogeneous yet diverse group of opinion makers, serving as a fair cross section of American journalism, is made up of representatives from both large metro dailies and small rural weeklies, including minority and ethnic publications and community business journals. Professionals from 31 states and the District of Columbia served as participants in the survey confined strictly to news release publicity for small business. For a complete survey and analysis of responses, send $8.95 plus $1.50 postage to Franklin-Sarrett Publishers, 3761 Vineyard Trace, Marietta, GA 30062 USA.

Dr. Jesse J. Lewis, Publisher
*The Birmingham Times*
Birmingham, AL

Robert Bryan, Publisher
*The Cullman Times*
Cullman, AL

Rick Thomason, Editor
*The Dothan Progress*
Dothan, AL

Bonnie Elsensohn, Editor
*Capital City Weekly*
Juneau, AK

Mike Patrick, Managing Editor
*Arizona Daily Sun*
Flagstaff, AZ

Jane Larson, Managing Editor
*Arizona Business Gazette*
Phoenix, AZ

John Genzabe, Editor
*The Business Journal*
Phoenix, AZ

Marian Frank, Business Editor
*The Phoenix Gazette*
Phoenix, AZ

Don Nicoson, Business Editor
*The Arizona Republic*
Phoenix, AZ

Bob Qualls, Editor
*The Baxter Bulletin*
Mountain Home, AR

Roger Morton, Editor
*The Auburn Journal*
Auburn, CA

Mike Stepanovich, Business Editor
*The Bakersfield Californian*
Bakersfield, CA

Larry Grooms, Editor-in-Chief
*Antelope Valley Press*
Palmdale, CA

Stephen Millard, Editor
*Park County Republican*
Bailey, CO

Ruth Zirkle, Editor
*The Gold Rush*
Cripple Creek, CO

Randy Sunderland, Editor
*Delta County Independent*
Delta, CO

Robert A. Hatch, Editor & Publisher
*The Lakeville Journal*
Lakeville, CT

John Coots, Publisher
*The Simsbury News*
West Hartford, CT

Denise Rolark Barnes, Managing Editor
*The Washington Informer*
Washington, DC

R. W. Nolte, Editor
*Hernando Today*
Brooksville, FL

Russell G. Boaeuf, Owner & Publisher
*Dunedin Times/Palm Harbor Sounder*
Dunedin, FL

Ben Eubanks, Editor
*Jacksonville Business Journal*
Jacksonville, FL

Kathy Blum, Editor
*Florida First Coast Homes*
Jacksonville, FL

Gail Newsome, Managing Editor
*The Jasper News*
Jasper, FL

Linda Thornton, Editor
*The Islander News*
Key Biscayne, FL

Russ Roberts, Executive Editor
*Lake City Reporter*
Lake City, FL

Eladio Armesto III, Publisher
*El Nuevo Patria*
Miami, FL

Joan C. Teglas, Editor
*The Floridian Newspaper*
Miami, FL

Tyler Ward, Business Editor
*Ocala Star-Banner*
Ocala, FL

Edward J. Foley III, Editor
*The Pompano Ledger*
Pompano Beach, FL

James M. Young, Acting Business Editor
*The Palm Beach Post*
West Palm Beach, FL

Portia A. Scott, Assistant to the Publisher
*Atlanta Daily World*
Atlanta, GA

Fran Rothbard, Managing Editor
*The Atlanta Jewish Times*
Atlanta, GA

Millann Travis Funk, President & Editor
*Atlanta Small Business Monthly*
Atlanta, GA

Jim Smith, Editor
*The Post-Searchlight*
Bainbridge, GA

Walter B. Geiger, Jr., Publisher
*The Herald-Gazette*
Barnesville, GA

Robert M. Williams, Jr., Publisher
*The Blackshear Times*
Blackshear, GA

Rhonda Vines, News Editor
*The Haralson Gateway-Beacon*
Bremen, GA

Waldo L. "Bo" McLeod, Publisher
*The Donalsonville News*
Donalsonville, GA

John R. Pool, Publisher
*Pickens County Progress*
Jasper, GA

David Bohanan, News Editor
*Banks County News/Jackson Herald*
Jefferson, GA

Steve Bills, Business Editor
*The Macon Telegraph*
Macon, GA

Curt Vincent, Managing Editor
*The Walton Tribune*
Monroe, GA

Kathy Pope, Editor
*The Monticello News*
Monticello, GA

Thomas Toles, Editor
*The Summerville News*
Summerville, GA

Cy Wood, Editor
*The Thomaston Times*
Thomaston, GA

Carl A. Miller, Co-Publisher/Editor
*The Idaho Business Review*
Boise, ID

Kirk Caraway, Editor
*Teton Valley News*
Driggs, ID

Robert M. Hammes, Editor
*The Gazette-Record*
Saint Maries, ID

David Keyes, Editor
*The Daily Bee*
Sandpoint, ID

Michael R. Montgomery, Editor
*The Telegraph*
Alton, IL

Geof Skinner, Editor
*The Gazette-Democrat*
Anna, IL

Wm. H. Schroeder, Publisher
*Lakeland Publishers, Inc.*
Grayslake, IL

James Kane, Business Editor
*The Daily Herald*
Arlington Heights, IL

Debra J. Harshman, Editor & Publisher
*The Paper*
Barry, IL

Kristin Gilpatrick, Editor
*Northern Ogle Tempo*
Byron, IL

Marta Foster, Editor
*El Heraldo de Chicago*
Chicago, IL

Rick A. Baier, Editor
*The News/Independent*
Cissna Park, IL

James C. Merkel, Columbia Editor
*Monroe County Clarion Journal*
Columbia, IL

Robert S. Kendall, Chairman
*Martinsville Daily Reporter*
Martinsville, IN

Norman Grissom, Publisher
*The Mitchell Tribune*
Mitchell, IN

Brian Walker, Editor
*The Muncie Evening Press*
Muncie, IN

Karen Fritz, Editor
*Pulaski County Journal*
Winamac, IN

Mark D. Griggs, Editor
*Atlantic News-Telegraph*
Atlantic, IA

Dirk Van Der Linden, Publisher
*The Belmond Independent*
Belmond, IA

Deirdre Cox Baker, Editor
*The Battendorf News*
Battendorf, IA

William C. Baker, Editor
*The Clinton Herald*
Clinton, IA

Mark S. Shearer, Editor
*The Columbus Gazette*
Columbus Junction, IA

Dan Field, Publisher
*Adams County Free Press*
Corning, IA

David Ruble, Managing Editor
*Charles City Press*
Charles City, IA

Elaine Armstong, Lifestyle Editor
*Clarinda Herald-Journal*
Clarinda, IA

Barbara Dorsey, Publisher
*Wright County Monitor*
Clarion, IA

Edwin J. Sidey, Editor & Publisher
*Adair County Free Press*
Greenfield, IA

A. J. Pinder, Publisher
*Grinnell Herald-Register*
Grinnell, IA

Charles P. Gonzales, President
*Guthrie Center Times*
Guthrie Center, IA

Ronald C. Slechta, Publisher
*The Kalona News*
Kalona, IA

Russell Ebert, Editor
*Van Buren County Register*
Keosauqua, IA

Richard Pratt, Editor
*The Journal-Express*
Knoxville, IA

Debbie Loger, Editor
*The Chronicle*
Odebolt, IA

Dave Martin, Managing Editor
*The Register*
Oelwein, IA

Carol Anderson, Editor
*The Chronicle*
Pella, IA

Mark Reinders, Business Editor
*The Sioux City Journal*
Sioux City, IA

Rudy M. Taylor, Publisher
*The Caney Chronicle*
Caney, KS

Karl K. Gaston, Publisher
*The Ellsworth Reporter*
Ellsworth, KS

Ray Call, Executive Editor
*The Emporia Gazette*
Emporia, KS

Kay Berenson, Editor & Publisher
*The Hays Daily News*
Hays, KS

George Statham, Publisher
*Kansas City Kansan*
Kansas City, KS

Murrel W. Bland, Editor
*Wyandotte West*
Kansas City, KS

Robert McQuin, Owner & Publisher
*The Kingman Journal*
Kingman, KS

Julie M. Vosberg, Managing Editor
*The Newton Kansan*
Newton, KS

Lonny Thiele, News Editor
*Linn County News*
Pleasanton, KS

R. M. Menard, Editor
*Northwestern Kansas Register*
Salina, KS

William M. Hays, Editor & Publisher
*Washington County News*
Washington, KS

James Travis, Editor
*The Smoke Signal*
Wamego, KS

Cecil H. Wilson, Publisher
*The Mountain Advocate*
Barbourville, KY

Jed Dillingham, Editor
*The Dawson Springs Progress*
Dawson Springs, KY

Clay Scott, Publisher/Managing Editor
*The Herald-News*
Edmonton, KY

David Greer, Editor
*The News-Enterprise*
Elizabethtown, KY

Terry O'Connor, Managing Editor
*Boone County Recorder*
Florence, KY

Tina M. Kunkler, Editor
*Larue County Herald News*
Hodgenville, KY

H. B. Elkins, Editor
*Citizen Voice & Times*
Irvine, KY

Ralph B. Davis III, Editor
*The Jackson County Sun*
McKee, KY

Pam Shingler, Executive Editor
*Appalachian News Express*
Pikeville, KY

Don Estep, Publisher
*The Whitely Republican News Journal*
Williamsburg, KY

Juanita Quaid, Editor
*Donaldsonville Chief*
Donaldsonville, LA

Lisa Bell-Burns, Editor-in-Chief
*Louisiana Weekly*
New Orleans, LA

Sandra Smith, Editor
*The Madison Journal*
Tallulah, LA

Harriet Melancon, Editor
*Vacherie Enterprise*
Vacherie, LA

Mary Valliant, Managing Editor
*Star-Democrat & Sunday Star*
Easton, MD

Andreae Downs, Co-Editor
*The Brookline Citizen*
Brookline, MA

Rachael Jarvinen, Editor
*South Shore News*
Rockland, MA

Dick Powers, Editor
*The Revere Journal*
Revere, MA

Bob Steensonn, Editor
*The Sentinel*
Fairmont, MN

Sarah Bondurant, Editor
*The Democrat*
Senatobia, MS

John Sullivan, Editor & Publisher
*The Livingston Enterprise*
Livingston, MT

Nancy Blair, Business Editor
*The Courier-Post*
Cherry Hill, NJ

Ward J. Miele, Editor
*Verona-Cedar Grove Times*
Verona, NJ

Gene Ballinger, Editor
*The Courier*
Hatch, NM

Brenda Masengill, Editor
*Hobbs Daily News-Sun*
Hobbs, NM

Walter Smith, Publisher
*New York Beacon*
Brooklyn, NY

Frederick Halla, Editor & Publisher
*The Brooklyn Record*
Brooklyn, NY

Charles Rogers, Managing Editor
*The Canarsie Courier*
Brooklyn, NY

Carla Cohen, Editor & Publisher
*The Floral Park Bulletin*
Floral Park, NY

Robert L. Frick, Deputy Business Editor
*The Democrat & Chronicle*
Rochester, NY

Holly Hall, Editor
*The Yancy Journal*
Burnsville, NC

Peggy K. Gosselin, Editor
*The Enterprise*
Canton, NC

Gary Cunard, Publisher
*Franklin Times*
Louisburg, NC

Randy Case, Publisher
*The Messenger*
Madison, NC

Lynn S. Carlson, Managing Editor
*The Brunswick Beacon*
Shallotte, NC

Dan Bender, Editor
*Greenfield Daily Times*
Greenfield, OH

Gloria Trotter, Editor & Publisher
*Countywide News*
Tecumseh, OK

Ray Lokey, Editor & Publisher
*Johnson County Capital Democrat*
Tishomingo, OK

Denny Bonavita, Managing Editor
*Courier Express*
Du Bois, PA

Paul Palange, Managing Editor
*The Evening Times*
Pawtucket, RI

Mark Hausman, Owner
*Hamlin County Herald-Enterprise*
Hayti, SD

Don Gerken, Managing Editor
*Pennington County Prevailer-News*
Hill City, SD

Dave Nelson, Staff Reporter
*The Hot Springs Star*
Hot Springs, SD

Bennie Scarton, Jr., Assistant Editor
*The Journal Messenger*
Manassas, VA

# Bibliography

1. Byrne, Robert. *The Third - And Possibly The Best - 637 Best Things Anybody Ever Said* . 1986, Atheneum, NewYork.

2. Killenberg, George M. and Rob Anderson. *Before The Story: Interviewing and Communication Skills for Journalists* . 1989, St. Martin's Press, New York.

3. Rosenblum, Mort. *Coups & Earthquakes: Reporting the World to America* . 2nd edition 1981, Harper & Row, New York.

4. Byrne, Robert. *The Third - And Possibly The Best - 637 Best Things Anybody Ever Said* . 1986, Atheneum, NewYork.

5. Killenberg, George M. and Rob Anderson. *Before The Story: Interviewing and Communication Skills for Journalists* . 1989, St. Martin's Press, New York.

6. Byrne, Robert. *The Third - And Possibly The Best - 637 Best Things Anybody Ever Said* . 1986, Atheneum, New York.

7. Flesch, Rudolf, Ph.D. *The Art of Readable Writing* . 1949, First Collier Books Edition 1962, Collier-MacMillan Canada Ltd., Toronto.

# Index